MATH
Skill Enhancement

Lloyd D. Brooks, Ed.D.
Memphis State University

PARADIGM

ABOUT THE AUTHOR

Lloyd D. Brooks is chair of the Department of Management Information Systems and Decision Sciences at Memphis State University. He received his undergraduate degree from Middle Tennessee State University and graduate degree from the University of Tennessee. He has researched and published widely in business math and computing, including several textbook and software publications in these areas. He has served as president of the Southern Business Education Association and has served on the executive board of the National Business Education Association. In addition, he was named Tennessee Business Teacher of the Year and National Data Educator of the Year in 1991.

Developmental Editor: Roberta Moore
Project Manager: Cynthia Miller
Designer: Joan Silver
Desktop Production: Kathleen Oftedahl
Cover Design: Pam Belding

Acknowledgements

We wish to thank the following instructors and technical experts
who contributed to this book:

Len Marachek
Hannepin Technical College
Eden Prairie, Minnesota

Karen Resnick
New York, New York

Library of Congress Cataloging-in-Publication Data

Brooks, Lloyd D., 1942-
    Math: skill enhancement / Lloyd D. Brooks.
      p. cm.

    ISBN 1-56118-261-3
    1. Business mathematics.   2. Business mathematics—
Problems, exercises, etc. I. Title.
HF5961.B7633 1993
650'.01'513—dc20

92-44949
CIP

ISBN 1-56118-261-3

© 1994 by Paradigm Publishing Inc., 280 Case Avenue, Saint Paul, Minnesota 55101

Printed in the United States of America
10 9 8 7 6 5 4 3 2 1

Contents

Preface

Introduction

This first edition of *Math for Workplace Success: Skill Enhancement* is designed to provide a series of practical problems in a problem-solving design. Over 80 percent of the examples are in a word problem format to provide problems related to the real world and to develop logical thinking skills.

This text is designed for student use. Although a majority of problems relate to a general business environment, settings and terminology relate to a wide variety of occupations. The content of the extensive word problems will generate interest and provide a stimulus for making students want to learn while using problem-solving procedures.

Text Design

Organization. The text contains 13 sections grouped into three units. A fourth unit provides extra practice and serves as a culmination unit of study. All problems are designed in a multiple-choice format.

Each section begins with a series of five problems that relate only to mechanics needed for making computations. While completing this series, the learner can readily determine whether or not a weakness exists relating to basic computation. This series is followed by 20 word problems that develop thinking skills.

Reinforcement. Students are provided with plausible alternatives for each problem. After completion of a problem, students can review the **Answers and Explanations** section in the back of the text for immediate reinforcement and/or explanation. If the problem is completed successfully, this section will indicate that the correct alternative has been selected for the problem. If a problem is not completed successfully, an explanation indicating why the alternative is incorrect will be provided. Procedures for completing the problem correctly are also provided.

This format presents a model approach for understanding appropriate procedures needed for completion of the problem and also helps develop good problem-solving techniques. The normal approach to follow while completing problems will be to solve the problem and then review the solution in the back of the text to confirm that a problem was completed successfully or to review an explanation that outlines procedures needed to complete the problem.

Calculator use. The format included in the **Answers and Explanations** section follows the one used to solve problems while using electronic calculators. However, use of calculators by students will be determined by the objectives of the instructor.

Instructional Approach

The format of the text is designed to permit completion of problems while using a self-paced approach or progressing at an individualized rate. Constant reinforcement is provided to help monitor the learning development stages.

The self-directed approach is facilitated by answers and explanations, which are included in the **Answers and Explanations** section at the back of the text. This feature provides immediate feedback relative to correct answers or explanations for problems where incorrect alternatives are selected.

Some aspects of group instruction can be incorporated into the learning process, if desired. If this combination approach is desired, general explanations can be provided at the beginning of each section and/or unit. Students will then progress at an individualized rate while completing problems in each section. A unit test for the first three units, which does not include answers in the back of the text, can then be used to measure competency levels.

Evaluation

Unit tests can be used for evaluation purposes. These tests can also be used to determine whether or not students have developed the needed skills. The extra practice exercises (Unit IV) can be used for making assignments to students needing additional skill development.

Educational Program Placement

This program is designed to be used in a wide variety of educational environments. Many adult education programs will find the program to be beneficial for refreshing or developing basic math skills. Vocational-technical programs will find the program to be beneficial for enhancing math skills (including remedial skills) needed in a wide variety of occupations. In these environments, the text can be used as a stand alone product or as a supplement to a program, such as *Math for Workplace Success* from Paradigm Publishing Inc. Postsecondary institutions will find the text to be beneficial as a basic skills enhancement to supplement the regular text, such as *Business Mathematics* available from Paradigm Publishing Inc., being used in the business math course. As indicated above, the text will be beneficial in almost any educational environment where a practical problem-solving approach is desired for enhancing basic math skills development or where a series of word problems is needed.

Final Note

Field tests with this text indicate that students can use the text to enhance basic math skills needed for workplace success. For learning environments with available microcomputer laboratories, a comparable math skills enhancement program is available from Paradigm Publishing Inc. in a microcomputer software format.

WORKPLACE PROBLEMS

PART ONE

SOLVING BASIC MATH PROBLEMS

Addition and Subtraction

The first five problems that follow are warmup exercises to give you a chance to practice basic math skills. You may use a calculator or paper and pencil. Circle the letter of the correct answer, and compare your answers with those found on page 135. If your answers are correct, go on to complete the problems in this section. If the answers you select are incorrect, try the problems again. If you continue to answer the questions incorrectly, see your instructor before attempting to complete this section.

1. Add: 32 + 2 + 45 + 124 = ?

   a. 200
   b. 203
   c. 204
   d. 206

2. Add: 348 + 476 + 628 = ?

   a. 900
   b. 985
   c. 1,241
   d. 1,452

3. Add: 1.278 + 1.03 + 1.2734 = ?

   a. 2.782
   b. 3.4217
   c. 3.5814
   d. 3.6214

4. Subtract: 877.28 – 76.78 = ?

    a. 800.5

    b. 800.05

    c. 795.5

    d. 792.05

5. Add: $875.82 + $89.32 = ? Then subtract: $79.89?

    a. $867.25

    b. $884.25

    c. $885.25

    d. $886.25

Read and solve the following problems. You will need to decide which basic math calculations are needed to solve each problem. Circle the letter of the correct answer from the choices offered. Only one answer is correct. Then compare your answers with those starting on page 135. When you select an incorrect answer, information will be given to help you learn how to solve the problem.

6. Three departments in the L & K Accounting firm are holding a meeting. An important 50-page report is needed for the meeting. One department needs five copies. Another department needs three copies. A third department needs seven copies. How many copies of the report are needed?

    a. 50

    b. 15

    c. 5

    d. 3

7. Review the following table of enrollment figures for City College. How many female students attend City College?

Class	Female	Male
Freshman	325	320
Sophomore	389	391
Junior	319	334
Senior	289	293

    a. 645

    b. 1,322

    c. 1,338

    d. 2,660

8. Review the following table of enrollment figures for City College. What is the total number of students who attend City College?

Class	Female	Male
Freshman	325	320
Sophomore	389	391
Junior	319	334
Senior	289	293

a. 645

b. 1,322

c. 1,338

d. 2,660

9. Jennie Switzer works for the Modern Design Florist Shop. Yesterday, she had sales in the following amounts: $123.45, $67.43, $29.29, $109.42, and $72.48. Her goal is to sell $400 each day. Did she meet her goal yesterday?

a. Yes

b. No

10. Brett Canty works as an inventory clerk at Jane Maguire's Computer Supply Store. The following table shows the number of ribbons on hand. When the total number on hand is less than 400 ribbons, Brett orders more. Does Brett need to order more ribbons?

Product No.	Ribbons on hand
#723Y	145
#712Y	107
#708	157

a. Yes

b. No

11. Art Chang, personnel director, gives all new employees a three-part test. Scores on the three parts of the test earned by the person hired were as follows: 28.05, 36.4, and 30.003. What was the employee's total score?

a. 97.453

b. 94.453

c. 94

d. 89.453

12. Jan Carson works for Underwood Consulting. Sally Underwood says, "Jan, how many hours did Bill Simmons work on the Harper account?" A review of the records showed that Bill worked the following hours: Monday, 6.5; Tuesday, 7.25; Wednesday, 8.5; Thursday, 7.75; and Friday, 8 hours. What was the total number of hours worked?

   a. 35.75

   b. 36

   c. 38

   d. 38.25

13. John Thompson is an assistant to Linda Gomez, who owns a manufacturing company. Ms. Gomez says, "John, I hope you can find a new printer and the supplies it needs for under $2,000." A catalog showed the following prices: printer, $1,899.75; toner, $79.28; and paper, $27.55. Was the total less than $2,000?

   a. Yes

   b. No

14. John Lewis works at City Garage. One of his jobs is to compute net pay (earnings less deductions) for employees. Robert Carson's payroll statement showed the following information: regular earnings, $872.45; overtime earnings, $75.89. Total deductions for the period were $147.25. What was the net pay for Robert Carson?

   a. $1,095.59

   b. $948.34

   c. $801.09

   d. None of the above

15. Rhonda Catlett works for Brad's Dry Cleaning Store. The supervisor, Ronald Timms, says, "Last week 3 employees at the South Street Store were out sick. I need to know the total number of employees who were at work every day last week at that location." What additional information will Rhonda need?

   a. The number of hours open each day.

   b. The time that the store opened each day.

   c. The number of branch offices located in the city.

   d. The total number of employees who work at the South Street location.

16. City Office Supply sells toner cartridges. The inventory sheet below shows the number of cartridges in stock on Monday and the number sold during the week. At the end of the week how many cartridges remain in inventory to be sold?

Inventory Sheet—AP209 Toner Cartridge	
Number available on Monday:	23
Number sold during the week:	4

   a. 27
   b. 23
   c. 19
   d. 4

17. Scott Flanagan is a sanitation engineer for City Office Supply. The owner, Sandra Lee, says, "Scott, you can retire from the company after working for 30 years." Scott has worked 19 years. How many years are left until Scott can retire?

   a. 49
   b. 30
   c. 19
   d. 11

18. George Prazma works as a production control clerk in a company that manufactures baseball gloves. The company normally produces 738 gloves per month and is open 6 days a week. George's weekly report shows 149 gloves produced so far this month. How many more gloves are needed to reach the monthly goal?

   a. 887
   b. 589
   c. 738
   d. 6

19. The week's payroll statement for Glynda Jefferson, who has worked at Automatic Gates, Inc. for 15 years, shows the following information: regular earnings, $589.24; overtime earnings, $72.45. Deductions were $41.50 for FICA taxes and $104.35 for federal withholding taxes. What is Glynda Jefferson's net pay?

   a. $515.84
   b. $661.69
   c. $145.85
   d. $807.54

20. Ralph Phillips is a salesperson for Schwartz Retailers. Monday, he made the following sales: $135.34, $275.34, $309.28, and $198.30. That day, two items were returned to the store for these amounts: $37.85 and $27.61. What were Ralph's net sales for the day?

   a. $918.26
   b. $852.80
   c. $65.46
   d. $983.72

21. Alice Jones works in a stock brokerage office. A client says, "The stock that I bought last year has increased in value. How much has it increased?" The purchase price of the stock was $37.875. Alice's computer shows that the current price is $52.5. What amount should Alice tell the client?

   a. $90.375
   b. $14
   c. $14.6
   d. $14.625

22. Herb Gentzel is a merchandising specialist for Santolini Electronics, Inc. His supervisor, Carolyn Hannah, says, "We sold a TV for $975.85 which cost $635.84 and a VCR for $307.50 which cost $189.75. Did we exceed a $450 profit?"

   a. Yes
   b. No

23. Brenda Moore is starting her own catering business. Her monthly bank statement shows a beginning balance of $875.92. There were two deposits, $275.89 and $304.55, and one $325.45 withdrawal (deduction). What was her ending checkbook balance?

   a. $325.45
   b. $1,130.91
   c. $1,456.36
   d. There is not enough information.

24. Thomas Benson, a sales representative at Holiday Motors, just sold a car for $12,389.25. Holiday purchased the car for $8,756.25. Thomas's sales commission was $123.89. What is Holiday's profit on the car?

   a. $3,509.11
   b. $8,880.14
   c. $3,633.00
   d. None of the above

25. Rosa Puente works part-time at the Speedy Bicycle Shop. Her supervisor, Berta Hart, says, "Our new bicycles cost us $289.45 and sell for $312.58 per bicycle. Our old bicycles cost us $274.85 and sold for $307.25 per bicycle. Which bicycles will result in the highest profit per bicycle?"

a. New bicycles
b. Old bicycles

Answers: Quick Check and Explanations, see page 135.

Multiplication 2

The first five problems that follow are warmup exercises to give you a chance to practice basic math skills. You may use a calculator or paper and pencil. Circle the letter of the correct answer, and compare your answers with those found on page 140. If your answers are correct, go on to complete the problems in this section. If the answers you select are incorrect, try the problems again. If you continue to answer the questions incorrectly, see your instructor before attempting to complete this section.

1. Multiply: 38 x $18 = ?

   a. $681
   b. $684
   c. $686
   d. $694

2. Multiply: 384 x $120 = ?

   a. $45,090
   b. $45,921
   c. $46,001
   d. $46,080

3. Multiply: 364 x 2.865 = ?

   a. 971.96
   b. 1,024.86
   c. 1,042.86
   d. 1,051.86

4. Multiply: 1,200 x $.75 = ?

    a. $900

    b. $902

    c. $903

    d. $904.75

5. Multiply: 750 x 0.006 = ?

    a. 450

    b. 45

    c. 4.5

    d. 4.05

Read and solve the following problems. You will need to decide which basic math calculations are needed to solve each problem. Circle the letter of the correct answer from the choices offered. Only one answer is correct. Then compare your answers with those starting on page 140. When you select an incorrect answer, information will be given to help you learn how to solve the problem.

6. The payroll form shown below shows the number of hours Jeannie Duvall worked last week and her hourly rate of pay. What were her earnings?

PAYROLL FOR WEEK OF _____		
Number of Hours	Hourly Pay Rate	Earnings
38	$15	_____

    a. $53

    b. $23

    c. $570

    d. None of the above

7. Barbara Jawolski is a data entry specialist for a public relations firm. She can keyboard 65 words per minute and can address 180 envelopes per hour. Her supervisor says, "We have a big mailing of 1,500 envelopes. Barbara, can you address the envelopes today in 8 hours?" Can she?

    a. Yes

    b. No

8. Claire Fuller works at the Jackson Chair Company. Her assembly line can manufacture 2 chairs per minute. How many chairs can they manufacture in 3 hours?

    a. 6
    b. 120
    c. 360
    d. None of the above

9. Robert Taylor is a purchasing clerk at Selesky and Co. A department head says, "We need 9 SX486 computers and we have $15,000 in the budget. Can we afford to purchase this equipment?" Robert calls a supplier and finds out that the model wanted costs $1,584 each. What answer should Robert provide?

    a. Yes
    b. No

10. Bill Floyd earns $7.00 an hour as an assistant auto mechanic. He says to the payroll clerk, "What will my earnings be for a 4-week period if I work 40 hours per week?" What steps will the payroll clerk follow to answer Bill's question?

    a. Multiply the earnings per hour by 40.
    b. Add the earnings per hour to the number of hours per week and then multiply this sum by the number of weeks.
    c. Multiply the hours per week by the number of weeks and then multiply this by the earnings per hour.
    d. Compute the sum of the earnings per hour plus the hours per week.

11. Harriett Brown works in a warehouse that ships about 24,000 boxes of personalized cards around the world each year. The shipping cost per box is $2.875. The office manager says, "Harriett, how much will it cost to ship 230 boxes of personalized cards?"

    a. $69,000
    b. $6,612.50
    c. $661.25
    d. None of the above

12. Harry Tollefson maintains a database for an engineering firm. The office manager says, "We enter about 1,800 sales records per day, 5 days a week. The weekly data entry cost is $600. A local company has offered to enter the records for $.075 each. Which method costs less?"

    a. The engineering firm
    b. The local company

13. Marilyn Gattis works as a cost accountant. Yesterday, her supervisor said, "Marilyn, our printer uses carbon ribbons which cost us $.10 per printed sheet. A laser printer will cost $.035 per printed sheet. If we print 5,000 sheets per month, what will our monthly printing cost be with the laser printer?"

    a. $350

    b. $500

    c. $1,750

    d. $175

14. Gerald Hauss is the payroll clerk at Barnes Manufacturing Co. One of the production employees, Russ Cochran, has decided to quit after eight years with the company. Russ is paid $.175 for each unit he produces. He has not been paid for his last 1,758 units. What amount should Gerald pay Russ?

    a. $30.76

    b. $30.77

    c. $307.65

    d. $3,076.50

15. Lee and Johns, a local legal firm, orders office supplies as shown on the order form below. What is the total amount of the order?

ORDER FORM

Date _____ Supplier _____

Quantity	Item	Price
30	Legal Pads	$.50 each
12	Computer Disk Boxes	$14.95 per box

Date Needed _____   Ordered by _____

Supervisor's approval _____

    a. $15.00

    b. $179.40

    c. $164.40

    d. $194.40

16. Gary Luster works at Raul's Office Supply. His supervisor, Judy Chism, says, "Gary, what is the total value of our inventory of cellophane tape? We sell about 4,500 rolls each month." Gary uses the computer to check the inventory. He finds that there are 11,245 rolls in inventory. If each roll costs $.50, what is the value of the tape inventory?

    a. $5622.50

    b. $562.25

    c. $2,250

    d. None of the above

17. Larry Holtzman is a marketing representative at the Wong Furniture Store. One of his customers wants to buy 3 Executive Chairs costing $339.95 each. This customer buys about $12,000 each year. What is the cost of this order?

    a. $12,339.95

    b. $1,019.85

    c. $339.95

    d. $10,980.15

18. Each year Brownstone Inns spends about $9,500 to buy computer paper. The office manager says, "I have found a store that will sell computer paper for $25.50 per case. We have used about $4,000 in computer paper so far this year. For the rest of the year we need 225 additional cases. How much money will this paper cost?"

    a. $5,500

    b. $13,500

    c. $5,737.50

    d. $1,737.50

19. Mable Yee works at Brownstone Inns, which uses about 7,500 pencils per year in guest rooms. The office manager says, "Mable, Ace Co. will provide us with 7,500 pencils for $4,000. Another supplier, Best Co., will provide the pencils for $.50 per pencil. Which supplier offers the lowest price?"

    a. Ace Co.

    b. Best Co.

20. Harold Washington works in the payroll department at a company that employs 300 people. A new employee will be paid $7.70 per hour. Although some employees work 40 hours per week, the new employee will work only 37.5 hours per week. What amount will the new employee earn each week?

   a. $308
   b. $1,500
   c. $288.75
   d. None of the above

21. Roberto Garcia works in the purchasing department at Upton Insurance Company. The purchasing director, Barbara Embry, says, "Roberto, one supplier will sell us #189Y policy forms for $.015 each. Another supplier has offered us 180,000 forms for $2,750 total. Which proposal offers the lowest price for 180,000 forms?"

   a. Forms for $.015 each
   b. Forms for a total price of $2,750

22. Howard Reaves is a resource analyst for a Los Angeles advertising agency. The firm occupies 15,782 square feet of office space; its rent is $.655 per square foot. The manager, Ned Cook, says, "Howard, a company in San Francisco will rent the same amount of space for $12,000. Which location offers the lowest cost?"

   a. Los Angeles
   b. San Francisco

23. Janis Crespi is a data entry clerk for Epson Truck Lines. She is paid $.075 for each record entered on the computer terminal. Yesterday, she entered 824 records. Experienced data entry clerks can enter as many as 1,200 records per day. How much did Janis earn yesterday?

   a. $90
   b. $61.80
   c. $618
   d. $900

24. Terry Burns works at Goode Health Care Center. The office manager says, "Terry, we use a daisy-wheel printer that costs $.10 per printed sheet. A new laser printer costs $.04 per page. What are the monthly savings if we print 5,000 pages during the month?"

    a. $500
    b. $300
    c. $200
    d. None of the above

25. A salesperson, James DuBois, at Lucia's Car Sales sold 6 cars last week for a $92,500 total sales amount. Salespersons are paid a $975 weekly salary or a commission equal to .015 times the total sales amount for the week. Which plan will provide Mr. DuBois with the highest salary?

    a. $975 weekly salary
    b. .015 commission

Answers: Quick Check and Explanations, see page 140.

Division

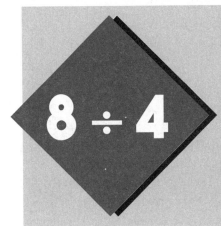

The first five problems that follow are warmup exercises to give you a chance to practice basic math skills. You may use a calculator or paper and pencil. Circle the letter of the correct answer, and compare your answers with those found on page 145. If your answers are correct, go on to complete the problems in this section. If the answers you select are incorrect, try the problems again. If you continue to answer the questions incorrectly, see your instructor before attempting to complete this section.

1. Divide: 444 / 6 = ?

   a. 7.4

   b. 74

   c. 76

   d. 76.6

2. Divide: 13,440 / 24 = ?

   a. 524

   b. 556

   c. 558

   d. 560

3. Divide: 900.75 / 2.5 = ?

   a. 3,603

   b. 1,936

   c. 360.3

   d. 360.25

4. Divide: 525.75 / 0.05 = ?

   a. 10,515

   b. 1,051.5

   c. 105.15

   d. 10.515

5. Divide: $6.75 / 150 = ?

   a. $.0015

   b. $.045

   c. $.15

   d. $45

Read and solve the following questions. You will need to decide which basic math calculations are needed to solve each problem. Circle the letter of the correct answer from the choices offered. Only one answer is correct. Then compare your answers with those starting on page 145. When you select an incorrect answer, information will be given to help you learn how to solve the problem.

6. Wayne Burton is a purchasing clerk at Carlyle Department Store. The store spends about $9,975 each year on printer ribbons. His supervisor says, "Wayne, I have $1,875 remaining in the budget for printer ribbons. If the ribbons cost $15 each, can we purchase the 150 ribbons we need to complete the year?"

   a. Yes

   b. No

7. Noah's Ark, a pet store that has been in operation for 3 years, keeps a record of the number of sales made each hour. Yesterday, 222 sales were made during the 6 hours that the store was open. The same number of sales was made each hour. How many sales were made each hour?

   a. 1,332

   b. 228

   c. 37

   d. 216

8. David Johnson is a shipping clerk at Royal Truck Lines. The freight manager says, "David, we have 1,152 cartons to deliver to the local warehouse. I hope this job can be completed tomorrow. I can get 64 cartons on a pallet. How many pallets will we need for all of the cartons?"

    a. 73,728
    b. 1,216
    c. 18
    d. 1,088

9. Ruaiz and Associates, a large market research firm, employs Gary Cobb as one of 12 accountants. The manager says, "Gary, we serve 6,720 customers across the country. If we employ 240 marketing representatives, how many customers should be assigned to each representative?"

    a. 560
    b. 28
    c. 20
    d. 6,960

10. Brunson Consultants offers seminars for computer training. Dennis Brunson, president, says, "Last year, we provided 32 seminars to 24 different businesses. A total of 960 participants attended these seminars. I need to know the average number of participants attending each seminar."

    a. 992
    b. 928
    c. 40
    d. 30

11. Brunson Consultants uses 3.5" disks for its 30 desktop computers. Disks are purchased in boxes, with 12 disks per box. A new catalog indicates that disks can be purchased for $18.72 per box. What is the cost per disk?

    a. $.624
    b. $224.64
    c. $30.72
    d. $1.56

12. Sarah Smith works at Downtown Cab Co. The owner says, "Our fleet of cabs averaged 16 miles per gallon of fuel last year. Cab #318 was driven 120,080 miles and used 7,600 gallons of gasoline. How did the miles per gallon or "mpg" for this cab compare with last year's average mpg?" What response should Sarah give to the owner?

   a. Cab #318 was higher than average

   b. Cab #318 was lower than average

13. Joe Silverman works for Dower Construction Co. His employer has 3,016 concrete blocks to deliver on a truck that can carry 377 blocks. He hands Joe a sheet of paper showing 3,016 being divided by 377 with an answer of 8 and asks Joe to check his answer. What should Joe do to check the computation?

   a. Multiply 8 by 377

   b. Divide 377 by 8

   c. Add 3,016 and 377

   d. Divide 3,016 by 377, then add 8

14. Bob Crawford works at du Mauriers's Candy Factory. His manager says, "Bob, I want to know our average expense for employee uniform laundry. Divide the total expenses by the number of employees to find the average." Expenses for the 4 employees were $158.50, $275.76, $190.50, and $165.40. What was the average expense?

   a. $790.16

   b. $3,160.64

   c. $197.54

   d. None of the above

15. Chris Destino is a payroll clerk at Worldwide Imports, which employs 42 persons. Allen Knowlton, one of the sales clerks, worked 52.5 hours and earned $462 last week. What were Allen's average hourly earnings?

   a. $11

   b. $8.80

   c. $19,404

   d. $504.00

16. David Ferguson works for Downy Enterprises. Maria Downy, president, says, "David, I want to provide a bonus to each of our 24 marketing representatives. There will be $55,646 in bonus money this year. What amount should be awarded to each of our marketing representatives?"

    a. $23,185.83
    b. $2,318.58
    c. $231.85
    d. None of the above

17. Lucy Chung, a testing specialist, gave an aptitude test to 5 applicants for a position. The scores were as follows: 56.8, 62.5, 58.2, 58.8, and 60.4. The manager says, "I will only interview applicants who scored above the average. How many persons will I be interviewing?"

    a. 1
    b. 2
    c. 3
    d. 4

18. The Copy Center has 12 boxes with 25 file folders in each. The office staff normally uses 40 file folders per week. How many weeks (rounded to one decimal place) will the existing file folders last?

    a. 7.5
    b. 1.6
    c. 3.3
    d. 12,000

19. Karl Maas manages a factory. He needs to know the labor cost for each unit of production. A production worker making $425.20 per week produces 25,500 items per week on the assembly line. What is the labor cost per item? (Round to 4 decimal places.)

    a. $1.6674
    b. $.1667
    c. $.0167
    d. $.0017

20. Tim Rutherford is an office clerk in a dental clinic. A dentist asks him to order 200 needles. The medical catalog shows that the needles can be ordered only by the dozen. How many dozen needles should Tim order?

   a. 16
   b. 17
   c. 12
   d. 20

21. Sonja Ecklund is a radio technician who earns $480 a week. She asks the payroll department to deduct 10 percent ($48) of her salary to be put in the employee stock fund. She wants to put $3,000 in the stock fund. How many weeks must she save to reach this goal?

   a. 96
   b. 48
   c. 300
   d. 63

22. Jay Hayes decides to contribute $.80 a week to the company gift account. However, he wants to stop the payroll deduction when his contribution reaches $98. How many weeks (rounded to one decimal place) will he need to contribute to reach his goal?

   a. 12.2
   b. 78.4
   c. 122.5
   d. None of the above

23. The word processing department at Blackburn Corp. tries to process text material at a cost of $2.25 or less per page. David Klatsch, a word processing specialist with a $315 weekly salary, formatted 150 pages of text material last week. Did David meet the productivity goal?

   a. Yes
   b. No

24. Yolanda Rodriguez is an office manager for a law firm. One of the law partners says, "I want to insure our computers. What is the average age of the 5 computers?" Yolanda determines that the ages are 4.6, 5.2, 4.8, 5.2, and 3.6 years. What is the average age?

   a. 5.12
   b. 5.08
   c. 4.78
   d. 4.68

25. Karen Dietz works for a printing company. Printer ribbons are purchased by the dozen. The manager says, "I need to know the cost per ribbon." Based on invoices from suppliers, Karen determines that 24 boxes cost $1,800. What was the cost per ribbon?

   a. $150
   b. $75
   c. $7.50
   d. $6.25

Answers: Quick Check and Explanations, see page 145.

Combination Problems 4

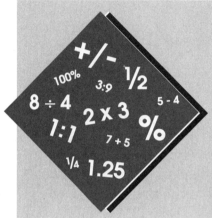

The first five problems that follow are warmup exercises to give you a chance to practice basic math skills. You may use a calculator or paper and pencil. Circle the letter of the correct answer, and compare your answers with those on page 150. If your answers are correct, go on to complete the problems in this section. If the answers you select are incorrect, try the problems again. If you continue to answer the questions incorrectly, see your instructor before attempting to complete this section.

1. Add: $34.45 + 3.8 + 7.002 = ?$

   a. 45.117

   b. 45.252

   c. 45.522

   d. 46.1002

2. Subtract: $17.5 - 2.07 = ?$

   a. 15.5

   b. 15.34

   c. 15.43

   d. 15.73

3. Add: $3.56 + 15.24 + 5.26 = ?$ Then subtract: $17.05 = ?$

   a. 6.17

   b. 7.01

   c. 7.1

   d. 7.11

4. Add: $35.78 + 24.62 = ?$ Then multiply by $2.5 = ?$

    a. 148.25

    b. 148.5

    c. 149

    d. 151

5. Divide: $525 / 25 = ?$ Then divide by $0.02 = ?$

    a. 10.5

    b. 105

    c. 1,050

    c. 1,050.2

Read and solve the following problems. You will need to decide which basic math calculations are needed to solve each problem. Circle the letter of the correct answer from the choices offered. Only one answer is correct. Then compare your answers with those starting on page 150. When you select an incorrect answer, information will be given to help you learn how to solve the problem.

6. Review the stapler sales table below. How many staplers were sold in total for the two months?

Stapler Sales

Month	Week 1	Week 2	Week 3	Week 4	Totals
Jan.	24	32	21	32	____
Feb.	12	8	23	20	____
Totals	____	____	____	____	____

    a. 172

    b. 109

    c. 63

    d. 36

7. The payroll clerk at Riverview Church is processing the musical director's paycheck. Her earnings are: regular salary, $572.35; overtime earnings, $23.89. Deductions are: FICA taxes, $37.56; federal withholding taxes, $107.25; state withholding taxes, $4.67. What is the musical director's net pay?

   a. $745.72

   b. $596.24

   c. $149.48

   d. $446.76

8. Grant Catalog Supply sells computer disks for $2.16 each. The disks are packaged with 10 disks in each box. City College ordered 14 boxes of disks. The catalog supervisor says, "City College has been a customer of ours for over 10 years. What is the total cost of their order?"

   a. $30.24

   b. $21.60

   c. $1.54

   d. $302.40

9. At City Office Supply, Anna Mak just marked the staples $2.23 per box. A customer says, "We use 3 boxes of staples every 2 weeks. I need enough for 24 weeks." How much will the staples cost?

   a. $53.52

   b. $160.56

   c. $80.28

   d. None of the above

10. Art Salvatorre, a customer, says to Anna Mak at City Office Supply, "I need 1,200 file folders for a 3-week project. How much will these folders cost?" The folders cost $.075 each and are sold only in boxes of 100. What price should Anna quote the customer?

    a. $900

    b. $90

    c. $300

    d. $16,000

11. Brimco Interior Decorators sold Bill Griego 2 executive chairs and 3 storage cabinets. The chairs sell for $339.95 each. The cabinets normally sell for $119.95 each, but are currently on sale for $99.95 each. A $40 delivery charge is added to all orders. What is the total cost of Bill's order?

   a. $979.75
   b. $679.90
   c. $939.75
   d. $1,019.75

12. Last week, Meryl Brunson worked 39 hours for $9.97 per hour at a local print shop. In order to earn more than she made at her last job, Meryl needs to make at least $390 per week. Did Meryl meet her $390 goal?

   a. Yes
   b. No

13. April Goode has worked as a barber for almost 20 years. A new employee, Tommie Brown, says, "I need to know the total price of these supplies. The catalog gives the unit price, but we need to order 75 items. What should I do?" What should April tell the new employee?

   a. Add the quantity and the unit price.
   b. Divide the quantity into the unit price.
   c. Divide the unit price into the quantity.
   d. Multiply the quantity by the unit price.

14. Last week, the amount of the payroll for the Fixall Auto Garage was $2,741.22. The garage has been in operation for 4 years and employs 9 persons. What is the average weekly pay of Fixall's employees?

   a. $304.58
   b. $24,670.98
   c. $685.31
   d. $76.15

15. Chan Wong is an office assistant for a law firm. She has a mailing of 2,812 letters to clients. Chan estimated that she can divide the work evenly among 4 secretaries by assigning about 700 letters to each secretary. Is this estimate correct?

   a. Yes
   b. No

16. Kathy Nelms is a purchasing clerk at the Modern Art Center. A manager calls her and says, "I need to spend the remainder of our supplies budget before the end of the year. We pay $.96 for 12 pencils, and we always need more pencils. How many can we order for $48.00?"

    a. 50
    b. 60
    c. 600
    d. None of the above

17. Ahmed Dostam works at Diskwrap Co., a compact disk packaging company. Ahmed packages about 9,600 disks per day on the assembly line. The company pays him $.0085 for each disk he packages. What is Ahmed's daily pay?

    a. $816.00
    b. $81.60
    c. $8.16
    d. $1,129,411.77

18. Clay Gilbert is an efficiency expert. His manager says, "Clay, I want to set standards for data entry. Larry Long is an average data entry clerk. He can input 212 characters per minute. If we use Larry as our standard, how many characters can we expect data entry clerks to input during each 8-hour day?"

    a. 12,720
    b. 1,590
    c. 101,760
    d. 1,696

19. Ignacio Morales is an accounting clerk in Diskwrap Company's payroll department. The vice president, Shirley Drummond, says, "I want to give our staff a bonus equal to their salary multiplied by .025. How much will that cost the company?" The total staff salaries are $820,824.80. What amount should Ignacio tell Ms. Drummond?

    a. $205,206.20
    b. $20,520.62
    c. $2,052.06
    d. $205.21

20. Cameraland Photography decides to expand. The company has $100,000 for salaries for new employees. Does Cameraland have enough money to add 4 new employees at $24,528.48 each?

    a. Yes

    b. No

21. Three departments at the Emery Construction Co. schedule a meeting. Expenses will be: $875.50, $1,045.78, and $843.55. The three departments will share the costs equally. How much will each department pay?

    a. 3

    b. $921.61

    c. $2,764.83

    d. None of the above

22. Klaus Schroeder is a clerk for Uptown Mortgage Co. A client, Mrs. Sen, has a mortgage payment of $725 per month for 30 years. She asks, "What will be the total amount of my payments over this period of time?" What amount should Klaus tell Mrs. Sen?

    a. $8,700

    b. $21,750

    c. $261,000

    d. None of the above

23. City College loans cars to staff to use on college business. The math department plans to send 2 professors to a Minneapolis conference, which is 875 miles one way. They can travel in the same car for 23.5 cents per mile. How much will the travel cost?

    a. $411.25

    b. $205.63

    c. $7,446.81

    d. None of the above

24. Jacob Stein works in a nursery for an hourly rate plus commission. He works 40 hours per week at $8.50 an hour. This week's commission is $75. What is Jacob's total pay for the week?

    a. $415

    b. $340

    c. $265

    d. None of the above

25. Marie Rymer is in charge of office supplies at a local construction company. She needs to order enough printer paper to have 30 boxes. Today, there are 7 boxes on hand from the previous order. The cost per box is $14.95. Marie orders the necessary printer paper. What is the cost of Marie's order?

   a. $343.85

   b. $104.65

   c. $448.50

   d. $553.15

Answers: Quick Check and Explanations, see page 150.

Unit I Test

1. Marilyn Brunson, a payroll clerk at Mike Murphy Construction Company, computes the weekly payroll. One of the carpenters had the following earnings and deductions during the past week. Earnings: $245.26 regular pay and $48.29 overtime pay. Deductions: $24.95, $7.47, and $13.56. What was the employee's net pay for the week?

   a. $45.98

   b. $247.57

   c. $293.55

   d. $339.53

2. Kimmie Ranshest works for the Madisonville Express. Mr. Lemonder says, "Kimmie, how many hours did Lawrence Riggs work on the Pennington special report?" A review of the records indicated the following hours: Monday, 4.5; Tuesday, 3.5; and Wednesday, 5.75. What was the total number of hours worked?

   a. 5.75

   b. 8.0

   c. 10.25

   d. 13.75

3. Aaron Donaldson is an administrative assistant for a law firm, Hall, Hall, and Diaz. During the past month he earned $2,234.38 in regular pay and $316.78 in overtime pay. His deductions for the same period were as follows: $128.95, $78.32, and $45.80. What was Aaron's net pay for the month?

   a. $2,504.22

   b. $2,551.16

   c. $2,298.09

   d. $253.07

4. Inez Harshman works for a local hospital. She has been employed there for six years. This past month she earned $2,539.28 in regular pay and $487.26 in overtime pay. Her deductions for this time period were as follows: $159.23, $68.24, and $72.60. What was Inez's net pay for the month?

   a. $2,726.47

   b. $3,026.54

   c. $272.65

   d. $3,326.61

5. City Bank establishes interest rates based on economic conditions. The bank offered a 10.54% interest rate yesterday. Today, the interest rate is 10.8%. What is the difference between the two interest rates?

   a. 21.34 %

   b. 10.26 %

   c. 26 %

   d. .26 %

6. Enrollment increased at Highmont High School last year by 6.94 percent. This year the increase in enrollment was 8.52 percent. What is the difference in the two percentages of increase?

   a. 1.85 percent

   b. 15.8 percent

   c. 15.46 percent

   d. 1.58 percent

7. Marta Henson is an inventory clerk for Johnson Building Supply Co. She notices that the supply of Renz Pens is low. These pens can be ordered in boxes of 144 pens per box. If she orders 18 boxes, how many pens will she get?

   a. 2,592

   b. 18,144

   c. 162

   d. 126

8. McReynolds Quick Stop orders drinking straws in large quantities. Straws come in boxes of 475 straws. If 12 boxes are ordered, how many straws will McReynolds have?

   a. 487

   b. 463

   c. 5,700

   d. 5,400

9. Howard Gregory works at Tufts Lumber Company. The owner, Susan Tufts, says, "Howard, I need to know the cost of ordering new filing cabinets for 13 of the 15 new employees hired last week." A supplies catalog lists each filing cabinet at a price of $124.28. How much will Ms. Tufts have to pay for the filing cabinets?

   a. $1,864.20

   b. $1,615.64

   c. $195.00

   d. $9.56

10. Margaret Morley works at Laura's Drapery Shop. The owner, Laura Krimpson, says, "Margaret, I need to know the cost of 15 fabric binders for employees to use for display." In the supply catalog the fabric binder is listed at $28.50 each. How much will Ms. Morley have to pay for the 15 binders?

    a. $42.75

    b. $427.50

    c. $43.50

    d. $420.00

11. Markus Pokorni is a data entry clerk for Swiftway Truck Lines. He is paid $.085 per record entered on the computer terminal. Today, he entered 810 records. How much did Markus earn today?

    a. $81.00

    b. $85.00

    c. $68.85

    d. $65.85

12. The owner of Crawford Products of Distinction, Mr. Don Crawford, says to the office clerk, "I have budgeted $978.36 for stationery and we need 120 boxes for our office staff. The stationery costs $7.89 per box. Can we purchase the needed stationery?" What answer should the office clerk give Mr. Crawford?

   a. Yes

   b. No

13. Every January Tennison Title Insurance Company gives each of their 93 employees a calendar desk mat, which covers the desk work area. This year, these mats can be purchased for $6.88 per mat. What will the total cost of the calendar desk mats be?

   a. $639.48

   b. $639.00

   c. $99.88

   d. $639.84

14. Brenda Green works part-time repairing computers. This week she worked 8 hours on Monday, 8 hours on Wednesday, and 6 hours on Friday. Her check stub showed that her gross pay for the week was $192.50. What is her pay rate per hour?

   a. $22.00

   b. $192.50

   c. $8.75

   d. $8.02

15. Cuong Nguyen works in the Computer Services Division of McNally Paper Products. The purchasing department needs to know how much the company is paying per box of standard computer paper. Mr. Nguyen recently purchased 48 boxes of paper for a total cost of $948.00. What was the cost per box of computer paper?

   a. $19.75

   b. $48.00

   c. $9.48

   d. $900.00

16. Ardis Phillips works part-time as a telephone operator for a department store. Last week she worked 5 hours on Monday, 6 hours on Wednesday, and 8 hours on Friday. Her payroll stub indicated that her gross pay for the week was $128.25. What is her hourly pay rate?

   a. $19.00
   b. $6.00
   c. $6.75
   d. $16.03

17. Samuel Gullini works at Lube and Go and his job is to compute net pay (earnings less deductions) for employees. The payroll statement for Eldon Heysek showed the following: Regular earnings, $859.43 and overtime earnings, $85.59. Total deductions for the period were $143.52. What was the net pay for Eldon Heysek?

   a. $945.02
   b. $801.50
   c. $229.11
   d. $715.91

18. Harriett Carter works in the Purchasing Department at Hart Computer Supplies. Mr. Hertz, purchasing director, says, "I noticed that we can buy a box of 12 computer disks for $6 or we can buy them individually for $.75 each. Harriett, what is the price for each disk if purchased by the box?"

   a. $.75
   b. $.50
   c. $62.00
   d. $4.50

19. The Bright Sun Day Care Center serves children from ages 2 through 5. Children presently attending are the following ages: 2, 2, 3, 3, 3, 3, 4, 4, 5, and 5. What is the average age of the children presently attending?

   a. 5
   b. 3.4
   c. 2.8
   d. 3

20. Miko Ashford works for Peppen's Pizza Delivery as a driver. In one evening, Miko drove the following numbers of miles on each delivery: 3.8, 5.6, 6.8, 7.8, 10.3, and 12.8. What was the average number of miles driven to make a delivery?

    a. 7

    b. 47.1

    c. 7.85

    d. 12.8

21. One of the partners in a law firm says, "I want to upgrade 5 of our old computers. Please tell me the average age of those machines." Inventory records show the ages are as follows: 4.8, 8.2, 6.8, 6.2, and 3.6 years. What is the average age of the computers?

    a. 29.63

    b. 6.832

    c. 6.73

    d. 5.92

22. Madelyn Harpison subscribes to an educational journal to stay up to date in her area of teaching. If the subscription rate for a 2-year period is $36, what is the monthly subscription cost for the journal?

    a. $2.00

    b. $1.50

    c. $18.00

    d. $1.80

23. Carlos Amarti had 24 reprints of a family photograph made at Dixie Photo Labs. The total cost for the photo reprints was $37.90. The basic fee for setting up the negative was $5.50. The remaining cost was for the 24 reprints of the negative. What was the cost for each reprint?

    a. $1.35

    b. $5.50

    c. $3.79

    d. $32.40

24. Randall Klinger works at Hemsley Rug Company. One of the production supervisors says, "If our assembly line can manufacture 4 oval bathroom rugs per minute, how many can we manufacture in 4 hours?"

    a. 960
    b. 16
    c. 240
    d. 64

25. Printer ribbons are purchased in boxes containing one dozen ribbons per box. Cindy McCoy works in the purchasing department. Mark Adkins, purchasing director, says, "I need to know the cost per ribbon." Cindy determined that 24 boxes were purchased for a $3,600 total cost. What is the cost per ribbon?

    a. $300
    b. $15.75
    c. $12.50
    d. $3.60

SOLVING RELATIONAL PROBLEMS

Fractions **5**

The first five problems that follow are warmup exercises to give you a chance to practice basic math skills. You may use a calculator or paper and pencil. Circle the letter of the correct answer, and compare your answers with those found on page 155. If your answers are correct, go on to complete the problems in this section. If the answers you select are incorrect, try the problems again. If you continue to answer the questions incorrectly, see your instructor before attempting to complete this section.

1. Reduce to lowest terms: 24/40 = ?

    a. 12/20
    b. 12/40
    c. 3/4
    d. 3/5

2. Add: 1/2 + 1/3 = ?

    a. 1/6
    b. 1/5
    c. 5/6
    d. 5/8

3. Multiply: $32,500 x 1/4 = ?

    a. $7,600
    b. $8,125
    c. $8,640
    d. $130,000

4. Subtract: 14 1/2 – 6 1/4 = ?

    a. 8 3/4

    b. 8

    c. 8 1/4

    d. 7 1/4

5. Multiply: 4 6/8 x 1/2 = ?

    a. 8 1/2

    b. 8 1/16

    c. 5 1/8

    d. 2 3/8

Read and solve the following problems. You will need to decide which basic math calculations are needed to solve each problem. Circle the letter of the correct answer, and compare your answers with those starting on page 155. When you select an incorrect answer, information will be given to help you learn how to solve the problem.

6. Chuck Barnes is an accounting clerk at Gifts of Distinction. The marketing manager says, "Chuck, our sales last year were $6 million. Of this amount, $2 million in sales were from outside the U.S.A. I expect sales next year to exceed $8 million. What part of our sales last year was from foreign countries?" (Answer in a fraction.)

    a. 3/1

    b. 1/4

    c. 3/4

    d. 1/3

7. Marilyn Bailey is the payroll clerk at a shoe factory. While processing the payroll, Marilyn noticed that of the 45 employees, 6 were absent last week. What fractional part of the employees were absent last week?

    a. 6/10

    b. 2/15

    c. 3/5

    d. 6/45

8. Mitzi Nomura is a clerk at a record store. A new employee says, "Mitzi, I can't remember the rule for reducing a fraction to lowest terms." What should Mitzi tell the new employee?

   a. Divide the numerator into the denominator.

   b. Divide the numerator and the denominator by the same number.

   c. Multiply the numerator and the denominator by the same number.

   d. Multiply the numerator by the denominator.

9. Family Services provides help to people in its community. Last year, donations to Family Services were $40,000. Of this amount, $14,000 came from private donations. The remaining $26,000 came from state and local governments. What part of the total money came from private donations?

   a. 13/20

   b. 7/20

   c. 7/13

   d. None of the above

10. Julia Robertson is a sales clerk with Goldstein's Department Store. She sometimes works on Friday nights and on weekends. She earned $18,000 regular pay and $6,000 overtime pay last year. What portion of her total pay was overtime pay?

   a. 1/4

   b. 3/4

   c. 1/3

   d. None of the above

11. Loren Obrinsky is a driver for a delivery company. The accounting clerk says, "Loren, we ordered 1,900 roses from our California supplier. What portion of the order has been delivered to our warehouse?" Loren found that 190 roses arrived yesterday and 190 roses arrived this morning. What portion of the total order had been delivered?

   a. 1/2

   b. 19/38

   c. 38/190

   d. 1/5

12. Calvin Watson, a recording technician, asks, "What part of my last year's pay went to pay income taxes? I think over one-third of my pay goes to these taxes." Payroll records showed $24,500 in total earnings and $6,125 in tax deductions. Did more than one-third go to income taxes?

    a. Yes
    b. No

13. Sang Lee is an admissions clerk at Hill Community College. The dean of students, Gary Ely, says, "Sang, our total enrollment is up 1/5 over last year. There are 625 freshmen and 450 sophomores enrolled in our programs. What portion of the total students is freshmen?"

    a. 1/5
    b. 25/43
    c. 18/43
    d. None of the above

14. Tony Fields works at Clark Community College. The dean of students says, "Applications for enrollment have gone up. The increase is at least 1/6 over last year. Out of 800 applications last year, 650 students enrolled. What portion of the students who applied actually enrolled in the school?"

    a. 1/6
    b. 3/16
    c. 65/80
    d. 13/16

15. Albert DeWitt works in the payroll department of the law firm of Henson, Thomas, and Lopez. On one case, Mr. Henson worked 16 hours, Ms. Thomas 9 hours, and Mr. Lopez 15 hours. Each attorney charges fees based on the portion of time he or she spends on cases. Mr. Henson says, "Albert, what portion did I contribute to the time our firm spent on the case?"

    a. 9/15 or 3/5
    b. 3/8
    c. 2/5
    d. 8/20 or 2/5

16. Ed Hoffman is a computer operator. His supervisor says, "Ed, you've done a good job for us this year. I am giving you a bonus equal to 1/10 of your salary." Ed's salary is $21,300. What amount will the bonus be?

    a. $2,130
    b. $213
    c. $213,000
    d. None of the above.

17. Paula Seals works at Broad Street Furniture Store. During the annual sale, items are being reduced by 1/4 off the original price. A salesperson says, "Paula, this customer purchased a sofa originally costing $440 and a chair originally costing $400." What steps should Paula take to compute the total amount due for the furniture?

    a. Add the total original cost of the two pieces of furniture. Multiply by 1/4 to find the discount amount. Subtract the discount amount from the total original cost.
    b. Add the total original cost of the two pieces of furniture. Multiply by 1/4 to find the discount amount. Add the discount amount to the total original cost.
    c. Add the total original cost of the two pieces of furniture. Multiply this amount by 4 to compute the discount. Then, subtract the discount from the total original cost.
    d. None of the above.

18. Benson, Carter, and Johns are partners in a construction company that builds houses. Benson and Carter each earn 1/4 of the profits. Johns earns 1/2 of the profits. Building the last house cost $121,100. It sold for $147,500. Benson's goal is to earn $6,500 or more on each house. Did he reach his goal?

    a. Yes
    b. No

19. Art, Mario, and Lewis Tornero combine their money to buy a print shop. Art contributes 2/5, Mario 1/4, and Lewis 7/20. They agree to share the profits based on the fraction of money each contributes. The print shop makes $62,000 the first year. How much is Art's share of the profit?

    a. $24,800
    b. $15,500
    c. $21,700
    d. $62,000

20. Bart Hillman works in a law office. An attorney says, "Bart, Mr. Jones died without leaving a will. Under the law, 1/2 of his 524-acre property, valued at $184,400, goes to his widow and the remainder is divided equally between his two children. How much money should each child receive?"

    a. $46,100

    b. $92,200

    c. $131

    d. None of the above

21. Thann Dihn works at a bank. A client says, "I want to buy a home. I earn $32,160 a year. What monthly payment can I afford?" The payment should not be more than 1/4 of the client's monthly earnings. What steps should Thann follow to determine the monthly mortgage?

    a. Multiply annual earnings by 1/4.

    b. Multiply annual earnings by 1/12.

    c. Multiply annual earnings by 1/12. Then, multiply this amount by 1/4.

    d. Divide annual earnings by 4/12.

22. Wanda Gross is a salesperson at East Furniture Center. A customer says, "Wanda, I like this cocktail table. I notice that the regular price is $680. Is it on sale?" All items in the store are reduced by 1/4. What price should Wanda give the customer?

    a. $680

    b. $170

    c. $510

    d. $850

23. Carrie Elston works in the personnel department at Raulston Electric. She gives all applicants an aptitude test of 240 questions. An applicant must answer 4/5 of the questions correctly to pass the test. Deana Canty missed 33 questions. Did Deana pass or fail the test?

    a. Pass

    b. Fail

24. Jim Kamura applied for a data entry job at Catalog Cameras. Jim inputs 90 characters per minute during a test. The supervisor says, "Jim, I suggest that you take a data entry course at Townsend College. You can increase your data entry speed by 2 1/2 times your current speed within 6 months." What will Jim's speed be after completing the training course?

    a. 180 characters

    b. 45 characters

    c. 225 characters

    d. None of the above

25. Darlene Fortner works at Castle Park Amusement Center. She is paid $8.60 per hour. Darlene worked 4 1/2 hours on Monday, 6 1/4 hours on Wednesday, and 3 3/4 hours on Friday. How much did Darlene earn for the week?

    a. $124.70

    b. $111.80

    c. $38.70

    d. None of the above

Answers: Quick Check and Explanations, see page 155.

Decimals 6

1.25

The first five problems that follow are warmup exercises to give you a chance to practice basic math skills. You may use a calculator or paper and pencil. Circle the letter of the correct answer, and compare your answers with those on page 160. If your answers are correct, go on to complete the problems in this section. If the answers you select are incorrect, try the problems again. If you continue to answer the questions incorrectly, see your instructor before attempting to complete this section.

1. Divide: $11.52 / 0.6 = ?

   a. $19.20

   b. $19.02

   c. $18.52

   d. $18.20

2. Multiply: $7,200 x 0.085 = ?

   a. $61.2

   b. $612

   c. $6,120

   d. $61,200

3. Add: 4.2 + 3.05 + 3 + 4.005 + 5.1 = ?

   a. 19.255

   b. 19.355

   c. 19.535

   d. 19.555

4. Subtract: 5.25 − 2.47 = ?

   a. 2.88

   b. 2.85

   c. 2.8

   d. 2.78

5. Multiply: $425.24 x 0.5 = ?

   a. $211.62

   b. $212.62

   c. $212.72

   d. $213.62

Read and solve the following questions. You will need to decide which basic math calculations are needed to solve each problem. Circle the letter of the correct answers from the choices offered. Only one answer is correct. Then compare your answers with those starting on page 160. When you select an incorrect answer, information will be given to help you learn how to solve the problem.

6. Martin Community College orders supplies from a mail order business. The catalog lists Pointex Pens for $5.76 a dozen. There is a postage charge of $.60 for each order of a dozen pens. A local supplier offered to sell the pens for $.55 each. Which source offered the lowest price?

   a. Mail order catalog

   b. Local supplier

7. City Office Supply advertises special sales by sending a flier to regular customers. Barbara Bates received the flier advertising legal pads at $6 for 12 pads. Barbara ordered 4 dozen pads. What is the cost of this order?

   a. $.50

   b. $24

   c. $6

   d. $48

8. Yvonne Delgado is a secretary for Norwood High School. Her principal, Anita Kirby, said, "Ms. Delgado, the chairs in our offices are worn out. Please order 5 new ones." The chairs cost $339.95 each. What is the total cost of the order?

   a. $1,699.75

   b. $344.95

   c. $334.95

   d. $67.99

9. Bertha Russell earned $875 for her last pay period with deductions of $48.75 for social security, $175.83 for income taxes, and $25 for savings. The average employee at her company earns $985 before deductions. What was the final amount of Bertha's paycheck?

   a. $249.58

   b. $1,124.58

   c. $625.42

   d. None of the above

10. A customer of Tilton Financial Services decided to buy some shares of stock. One of the stocks that he plans to purchase is selling for $89.375 per share. The customer decided to invest $1,251.25 in this stock. How many shares of stock can he purchase (rounded to even shares)?

   a. 14

   b. 111,830

   c. 1,162

   d. 1,341

11. John Schmitt works for Parton Appliance Center. The owner asks John to check on the cost of fire insurance premiums for the company. Mr. Parton suggested that the store be insured for $180,000. John found that the lowest rate was $.00295 per dollar of insurance coverage. What is the premium amount?

   a. $531

   b. $53,100

   c. $5,310

   d. None of the above

12. Disks by Mail, Inc. is a mail order company that sells compact disks. Mr. Olsen ordered 3 disks. Each disk cost $11.99. Shipping and handling charges must be added. Shipping charges are $1.29 for the first disk and $.42 for each additional disk. What is the total cost of the order?

   a. $13.28

   b. $33.84

   c. $35.97

   d. $38.10

13. Toys-R-Fun carries a wide range of toys. The stock of one product, Commando Jimmy, is running low. This product can be ordered only in sets of 6. Each Commando Jimmy costs $18.00. The inventory supply report showed that 9 items need to be ordered. What will the order cost?

   a. $216

   b. $162

   c. $972

   d. $12

14. Thrifty City, a discount store, often runs special sales to attract customers. Jolly bathroom tissue normally sells for $1.45 per package. During a special sales promotion, the tissue costs $4 for 3 packages. Belinda O'Connor purchased 12 packages. What was her total savings?

   a. $5.33

   b. $17.40

   c. $16.00

   d. $1.40

15. Paul Cranford's cousin lives in a distant city. On a map, the distance between the two cities is 2.5 inches. The scale of the map shows .5 inch equal to 100 actual miles. How far apart are the two cities?

   a. 250 miles

   b. 50 miles

   c. 500 miles

   d. 200 miles

16. The owner of a pet store decided to expand the store. A blueprint shows the expansion area as 4.75 inches. The blueprint scale shows, .25 inch on the blueprint plan as equal to 1 foot of actual expansion space. Will 20 feet of actual expansion space be enough?

    a. Yes

    b. No

17. Dover Telecommunications employs over 200 people. Employees get 0.5 vacation days for each 2 weeks of employment with the company. Nancy Fields has worked as a receptionist for the company for 10 years. How many vacation days does Nancy earn each year (52 weeks)?

    a. 4

    b. 13

    c. 26

    d. 104

18. Pride Real Estate orders about 184 memo pads for an 8-week supply. The company also orders 50 boxes of envelopes and 8 boxes of computer disks. Memo pads sell for $.45 each and a box of envelopes costs $.75. Computer disks cost $14.95 per box. Shipping costs will be $20. What will the order cost?

    a. $239.90

    b. $299.90

    c. $219.90

    d. $259.90

19. Ari Mecouri works at a local music store and needs to order folders. Folders can only be ordered in groups of 50 folders per box. Each box costs $4. He needs to order enough for the remainder of the month, which he estimates will be 400 folders. Will $35 from the petty cash fund be enough to pay for this order?

    a. Yes

    b. No

20. Vicki Fong works at a card and gift wrap store. The store's monthly spending budget is $568.65 It uses 90 rolls of gift wrapping paper. A local supplier provides gift wrapping paper for $5.85 per roll. Can Terri order the needed number of rolls within the store's monthly budget?

   a. Yes

   b. No

21. Tom Running Bear manages the Soft Rock Cafe. The cafe serves 200 rolls a day. A local baker provides rolls at 12 for $.96, if at least 100 or more rolls are bought. How much will the 200 rolls cost?

   a. $16

   b. $2,500

   c. $192

   d. None of the above

22. Ken Lasater is a receptionist at a dentist's office. Ken collects the money for the employee's snacks. One employee gave Ken a $20 bill to cover the cost of a $2.85 sandwich and a $.75 soft drink. How much change should Ken give the employee?

   a. $16.40

   b. $3.60

   c. $23.60

   d. None of the above

23. Alice Thompson is a clerk for Bartlett Office Supply. A customer received 5 cases of computer paper totaling $127.50. He returned 1 case of the computer paper because it was damaged. The customer requested a refund for the damaged case. What is the amount of the customer's refund?

   a. $127.50

   b. $25.50

   c. $102

   d. $153

24. Mario Ponti is a shipping clerk for Pazzazz Pen Co. A customer ordered 50 boxes of pens totaling $140.40. The customer returned 6 boxes of the pens. What should Mario do to figure out the refund amount?

   a. Divide the total cost by the number of boxes purchased. Then, multiply the result by the number of boxes returned.

   b. Add the cost of one box of pens to the total invoice amount.

   c. Subtract the cost of one box of pens from the total invoice amount.

   d. Multiply the cost by the number of boxes of pens.

25. Opal Sweetwater is an insurance adjuster who was asked to estimate the cost of replacing items damaged by a roof leak. She found that there were 175 file folders (costing $56 total), 45 memo pads (costing $22.50 total), 4 executive chairs (costing $339.95 each), and 10 boxes of clasp envelopes (costing $60 total) damaged by the water. What will it cost to replace the damaged items?

   a. $1,359.80

   b. $339.95

   c. $1,498.30

   d. None of the above

Answers: Quick Check and Explanations, see page 160.

Percents

The first five problems that follow are warmup exercises to give you a chance to practice basic math skills. You may use a calculator or paper and pencil. Circle the letter of the correct answer, and compare your answers with those on page 165. If your answers are correct, go on to complete the problems in this section. If the answers you select are incorrect, try the problems again. If you continue to answer the questions incorrectly, see your instructor before attempting to complete this section.

1. Change to a percent: 1/4 = ?

    a. 1/4 percent
    b. 40 percent
    c. 25 percent
    d. 12.5 percent

2. Change to a percent: 48/120 = ?

    a. 48 percent
    b. 40 percent
    c. 12 percent
    d. 4 percent

3. Multiply: 800 x 7.5 percent = ?

    a. 60
    b. 600
    c. 6,000
    d. 7,580

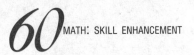

4. Change to a percent: 0.1285 = ?

   a. 1,285 percent

   b. 128.5 percent

   c. 12.85 percent

   d. 1.285 percent

5. Multiply: $26,800 x 8.25 percent = ?

   a. $2,580

   b. $2,211

   c. $2,208

   d. $2,125

Read and solve the following problems. You will need to decide which basic math calculations are needed to solve each problem. Circle the letter of the correct answers from the choices offered. Only one answer is correct. Then compare your answers with those starting on page 165. When you select an incorrect answer, information will be given to help you learn how to solve the problem.

6. Hal Thompson was offered a job as Sales Manager at Fern's Greenhouse at a monthly take home salary of $1,600. He decided he could afford to take the job if he budgeted $600 a month for rent, $350 for car expenses, $100 a week for living expenses, and the rest for savings and miscellaneous. Hal's father said, "Make sure you're not paying more than 25 percent of your salary for rent. If you are, you should think about finding a cheaper place to live." Does Hal need to consider moving to a less expensive apartment?

  a. Yes

  b. No

7. Evelyn Childs received a notice that her monthly installment payment for her furniture was overdue. The statement indicated that if the payment was not received in 10 days, Evelyn would have to pay a 2.5 percent late fee. On a balance of $922.40, what would be the late charge on Evelyn's account?

   a. $230.06

   b. $ 23.06

   c. $945.46

   d. None of the above.

8. Jeffrey Cho owns an accounting firm. Of 32 people who work for him, 8 are eligible for retirement. A goal is to have no more than 30 percent of the total employees eligible for retirement within the next 5 years. Employees can retire after 30 years of service or after reaching the age of 55. Is the percent eligible higher than the goal?

   a. Yes

   b. No

9. Bobby Joe Royal is a payroll clerk. His supervisor asked for a report on absenteeism. Bobby Joe found that within a period of 480 working days, 24 days were missed by all employees combined. An absentee rate of 6 percent or less is acceptable. Is the absentee rate for the 480-day period higher or lower than the acceptable standard?

   a. Higher

   b. Lower

10. Janet Baker works at Morrell Building Supply. The owner asked, "Janet, what percent of our overdue accounts are 90 days or more overdue?" Janet found the following information: $40,000 overdue less than 30 days; $20,000 overdue more than 30 days, but less than 90 days; and $20,000 overdue 90 days or more. What percent should Janet report to Mr. Morrell?

    a. 75 percent

    b. 25 percent

    c. 125 percent

    d. None of the above

11. Sal Vito works at Tower Office. Total expenses for the previous month were $180,000. Of this amount, $117,000 was used for salaries. His supervisor requested that Sal find the percent of money the company used for salaries. What percent should Sal report to his supervisor?

    a. 6.5 percent

    b. 65 percent

    c. 0.65 percent

    d. 35 percent

12. Vernon Spence works at Exotic Imported cars. Operating expenses for the previous month were as follows: salaries, $128,000; supplies, $12,800; and building and maintenance, $19,200. His supervisor, Ginger Coggins, asked for the percent of expenses for supplies. What percent should Vernon report to Ms. Coggins?

   a. 92 percent

   b. 80 percent

   c. 0.8 percent

   d. 8 percent

13. Marvin Weber works for Sanders Manufacturing, Inc., which makes a part for electronic equipment. Of 500 completed parts, 1 part was broken. Marvin was asked to find the percent of broken parts. Is this an acceptable level of production quality?

   a. Yes

   b. No. Only 100 percent is acceptable.

   c. Yes, because the part is hard to make.

   d. Information is not provided on production quality standards.

14. Dora's Desktop Publishing, Inc. provides desktop publishing services. All work is printed on laser printers. At the beginning of the month, there were 120 toner cartridges in stock. At the end of the month, 72 toner cartridges were in stock. What percent of the toner cartridges were used during the month?

   a. 72 percent

   b. 60 percent

   c. 48 percent

   d. 40 percent

15. Yoshi Miura works at Jernigan Shoe Store. His supervisor asks, "What percent of sales are made on Saturdays?" Yoshi totaled the amount of sales. The results were as follows: Monday, $1,198; Tuesday, $1,231; Wednesday, $1,210; Thursday, $1,317; Friday, $1,476; and Saturday, $1,568. What percent should Yoshi report to his supervisor?

   a. 19.6 percent

   b. 196 percent

   c. 1.96 percent

   d. None of the above

16. Colleen Grishom works for the post office. Colleen is a single mother with one child. She is saving for her child's college education by placing 5 percent of her $465.80 weekly net salary in a savings account. What amount is placed in the college savings fund?

    a. $2.33
    b. $93.16
    c. $460.80
    d. $23.29

17. Myra Dell is an accountant. Her annual earnings last year were $28,540.50. At the end of the year, Myra got a 6 percent raise. Myra had hoped for a $1,700 raise. Did the raise meet Myra's expectations?

    a. Yes
    b. No

18. John Lange is a systems analyst for Fairyland Hotels. His annual salary is $36,000. He receives an equal portion of this salary each month. John is offered a chance to transfer to San Francisco. If he agrees to the transfer, he will be given an 8 percent raise. What is the monthly amount of John's raise?

    a. $2,880
    b. $3,000
    c. $288
    d. $240

19. Paul DeSantis is a systems analyst for Taco Whistle Restaurants. He earns a $34,600 annual salary. He receives an equal portion of his salary each month. Paul's boss asked him to transfer to Charlotte, North Carolina. If he agrees to the transfer, he will be awarded a 7.5 percent raise. What is the dollar amount of Paul's annual salary after the raise?

    a. $2,595
    b. $37,195
    c. $32,005
    d. $34,600

20. One of the employees at the Adamson Museum of Colonial Times, Tim Hardaway, is awarded a weekly raise of $52.20. This amount will be added to his weekly salary of $580. Tim says, "I am not sure about my raise. The amount sounds low. I think the 8 percent raise I was awarded last year was higher." Which year did Tim receive a higher raise?

   a. Last year
   b. This year

21. Mikki Duffey is a production assistant for a music recording company. She has been with the company for 5 years and earned $22,000 last year. She recently received a raise. Mikki's new salary will be $23,760. What was the percent of her raise?

   a. 92 percent
   b. 80 percent
   c. 8 percent
   d. 0.08 percent

22. John Harrison is a salesperson at Briley Automotive Sales. He earns a commission on each sale. Yesterday he sold a used car for $8,660. The commission was $108.25. What was the commission percent?

   a. 0.0125 percent
   b. 0.125 percent
   c. 1.25 percent
   d. 12.5 percent

23. Hal Kondal works in the Brown Bear bookstore. A new book, *Computer Games,* just arrived in the store. The manager asked Hal to add 22 percent to the cost of the book to find the sale price. From the invoice Hal saw that the publisher charged $22.50 for the book. What should the bookstore price for the book be?

   a. $4.95
   b. $27.45
   c. $17.55
   d. $22.50

24. Jenny Brown currently earns $26,800 for her job as a word processing specialist. This year she will receive a 6.25 percent raise. What will her salary be after the raise?

    a. $1,675
    b. $25,125
    c. $28,475
    d. $43,550

25. James Langston, a customer at Haas Jewelry Store, made a $300 payment on his $5,000 account. The billing department requires that 10 percent of the amount due on an account be paid if the balance is over $3,000. Did Mr. Langston pay the correct amount?

    a. Mr. Langston paid over 10 percent of his bill.
    b. Mr. Langston paid exactly 10 percent of his bill.
    c. Mr. Langston's payment must be $500 higher.
    d. Mr. Langston's payment must be $200 higher.

Answers: Quick Check and Explanations, see page 165.

Ratios and Proportions

1:1

The first five problems that follow are warmup exercises to give you a chance to practice basic math skills. You may use a calculator or paper and pencil. Circle the letter of the correct answer, and compare your answers with those on page 170. If your answers are correct, go on to complete the problems in this section. If the answers you select are incorrect, try the problems again. If you continue to answer the questions incorrectly, see your instructor before attempting to complete this section.

1. Provide the ratio: 48 to 4 = ?

   a. 43:1

   b. 12:1

   c. 4:1

   d. 2:1

2. Provide the ratio: 195 to 15 = ?

   a. 19.5:1

   b. 15:1

   c. 13:1

   d. 7:2

3. Provide the ratio: 84 to 21 = ?

   a. 8:1

   b. 4:1

   c. 2:1

   d. 1.5:1

4. Supply the missing value in this proportion: 1/4:?/12

   a. 4

   b 3

   c. 2

   d. 1

5. Supply the missing value in this proportion: 2/$27:?/$270

   a. 20

   b. 27

   c. 54

   d. 135

Read and solve the following problems. You will need to decide which basic math calculations are needed to solve each problem. Circle the letter of the correct answer from the choices offered. Only one answer is correct. Then compare your answers with those starting on page 170. When you select an incorrect answer, information will be given to help you learn how to solve the problem.

6. Berl Distributors, Inc. offers training seminars for their marketing staff. A seminar scheduled 60 days ago for 30 marketing representatives is planned for next week. Motivational Consultants will provide 2 instructors. What is the participant-to-instructor ratio for the seminar?

   a. 60:2

   b. 30:1

   c. 30:2

   d. 15:1

7. Miracle Marketing establishes quotas for its 30 marketing representatives. The sales manager asks, "What was the ratio of our total number of marketing representatives to the number reaching their quotas last month?" Six of the marketing representatives reached their quotas. What procedure should be followed to determine the ratio?

   a. Compare the number of marketing representatives to the number reaching the quota.

   b. Compare the number reaching the quota to the value 1.

   c. Compare the total number of marketing representatives to the value 1.

   d. None of the above.

8. Many companies provide their marketing representatives and managers with automobiles. At Mircle Marketing 16 of the 48 marketing representatives and managers are furnished with company cars. What is the ratio of employees to furnished automobiles?

   a. 16:1
   b. 3:1
   c. 16:48
   d. 48:16

9. Martin Thompson is a research specialist with Miracle Marketing, which has offices in 18 states. There are 4 marketing representatives in Texas. Sales last month by the 4 Texas representatives were: 12, 8, 24, and 4. What is the ratio of total sales to marketing representatives in Texas?

   a. 9:2
   b. 48:1
   c. 12:1
   d. 48:4

10. Martha Aguilar works in the personnel department. She gives keyboarding tests to applicants. On one 3-minute test, the applicant keyed 150 words. Applicants must have a words-to-minutes ratio of at least 40:1. Did the applicant pass the test?

    a. Yes
    b. No

11. Bernie King is one of 3 shipping clerks working at Power Paper Company. Bernie received a shipping order for 180 reams of paper. The paper is shipped in 15 boxes. What is the ratio of reams of paper to a box?

    a. 15:1
    b. 12:1
    c. 5:1
    d. None of the above

12. Don Crawford works at Aqua Speed Boat Center. The manager asks, "Don, what is the ratio of new boats to used boats sold during the past 2 months?" Don found that 8 used boats and 16 new boats were sold this month. He found that 6 used boats and 26 new boats were sold last month. What is the ratio of new boats to used boats sold?

    a. 2:1
    b. 3:1
    c. 42:1
    d. None of the above

13. Nadine Yamaguchi works for Lightning Electronics. The manager says, "Check Charles Scrugg's records and find the ratio of the number of work days to the number of sick leave days. A 15:1 ratio is acceptable." Nadine finds that Charles Scruggs has been absent 18 days and present 234 days. Is this ratio acceptable to the manager?

    a. Yes
    b. No

14. Larry Krupski works at Hudson Manufacturing Company. There are 4 supervisors at the plant. The first assembly line has 8 employees. A second assembly line has 10 employees. The third assembly line has 10 employees. The plant manager asks, "Larry, what is the ratio of employees to supervisors at the plant?"

    a. 8:4
    b. 3:1
    c. 28:1
    d. None of the above

15. Joan Holt is a dentist at Dynamic Dental Clinic. She thinks that her patient load is too high. In one week Dr. Holt sees 105 patients, Dr. Kennedy sees 89 patients, and Dr. Jackson sees 112 patients. Is Dr. Holt's doctor-patient ratio higher or lower than the combined ratios for the three dentists?

    a. Higher
    b. Lower

16. Fred Hampton ordered 45 boxes of paper clips. No price was listed, so Fred must find the price. The catalog shows paper clips priced 5 boxes for $3. What proportion below will help Fred find the price of 45 boxes?

   a. 5/$3:45/$?

   b. 45/?:5/$3

   c. $3/5:45/$?

   d. None of the above

17. Dean Myers is asked to find out if space is available for expansion at Carpenter Electronics. His supervisor says, "Three wrapping machines require 28 square meters. We have 118 square meters of space available. Dean, will this be enough for 12 wrapping machines?"

   a. Yes

   b. No

18. Frank Kaiser is one of 6 office clerks at Richard's Manufacturing. Eighteen production workers produce 72 items in one hour. His supervisor wants to increase production to 140 items per hour. How many total employees should Frank recommend be employed to meet the increased demand?

   a. 4

   b. 560

   c. 35

   d. None of the above

19. Gina Bocaccio works at Lou's Lumber Co. A builder needs plywood for a roof. Based on the blueprint, 17 sheets of plywood will cover 238 square feet of the roof. Plywood is needed to cover 322 square feet. There are 25 sheets in inventory. Is this amount enough to meet the building needs?

   a. Yes

   b. No

20. Sam Wyche works at a clothing store. A customer says, "Mr. Wyche, I saw in the morning newspaper you are offering dress shirts at a price of 2 shirts for $37, including tax. I have been waiting for 6 months for these shirts to go on sale. How many shirts can be purchased for $370?"

    a. 20

    b. 10

    c. 6,845

    d. None of the above

21. Georgia McDonald is a process control clerk at Boyle Canneries. Labeling mistakes have occurred on 15 cans out of 7,500 cans processed. The shift foreman says, "Georgia, if this same rate of error is maintained, how many cans will have been processed when we reach 90 labeling mistakes?"

    a. 500

    b. 1,350

    c. 45,000

    d. None of the above

22. Joe Otto is a business major at City College. He works part-time at the Latino Museum. The curator asks, "Will we be able to provide tours for at least 500 people in a 9-hour day?" Joe found that 90 people can tour the museum during a 1 1/2-hour period. What answer should Joe give the curator?

    a. Yes

    b. No

23. Judy Munger works at City Cab. The owner says, "Judy, each of our cabs is driven approximately 84,000 miles each year. About how many gallons of gasoline will they use in a year?" A typical cab was driven 6,000 miles last month and used 400 gallons of gasoline. What response should Judy give to the owner?

    a. More than 5,000 gallons

    b. Exactly 5,000 gallons

    c. Less than 5,000 gallons

    d. More data are needed to provide an estimate.

24. Mike Carter is an insurance clerk for Bradford Insurance Services. Bradford pays 80 percent of a client's bill. The amount Bradford paid for Bill Turnbow's recent health problems was $840. What is the total amount of Mr. Turnbow's bill?

    a. $1,050

    b. $672

    c. $1,512

    d. None of the above

25. Ted Rotella works at Financial Planning Services. A client with $4,000 monthly income was paying $1,200 per month on a home mortgage. Ted knows monthly mortgage payments should equal 25 percent or less of the total monthly earnings. Is the client's monthly income sufficient to support the home mortgage payment?

    a. Yes

    b. No

Answers: Quick Check and Explanations, see page 170.

Combination Problems

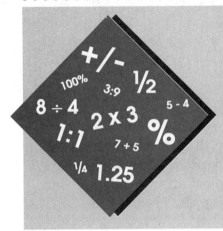

The first five problems that follow are warmup exercises to give you a chance to practice basic math skills. You may use a calculator or paper and pencil. Circle the letter of the correct answer, and compare your answers with those on page 175. If your answers are correct, go on to complete the problems in this section. If the answers you select are incorrect, try the problems again. If you continue to answer the questions incorrectly, see your instructor before attempting to complete this section.

1. Multiply: 1/4 x $28.64 = ?

   a. $7.16
   b. $28.64
   c. $114.56
   d. $428.64

2. Divide: $64.20 / 0.005 = ?

   a. $12.84
   b. $128.40
   c. $1,284
   d. $12,840

3. Multiply: $56.24 x 25 percent = ?

   a. $14.60
   b. $14.06
   c. $13.06
   d. $13.04

4. Multiply: $735 x 28.2 percent = ?

   a. $207.27
   b. $207.72
   c. $208.72
   d. $208.27

5. Provide the ratio: 64 to 24 = ?

   a. 24:1
   b. 8:3
   c. 8:1
   d. 7:3

Read and solve the following questions. You will need to decide which basic math calculations are needed to solve each problem. Circle the letter of the correct answer from the choices offered. Only one answer is correct. Then compare your answers with those starting on page 175. When you select an incorrect answer, information will be given to help you learn how to solve the problem.

6. Design Printing's employees are listed below. What portion of the employees are male? Answer should be expressed in a fraction.

EMPLOYEE LISTING		
Dunn — Male	Goodson — Female	Jen — Female
Everly — Female	Goodson — Female	Perez — Female
Fults — Female	Howe — Male	Woods — Male

   a. 3/6
   b. 3/9
   c. 1/3
   d. 1/2

7. Joan Whitmire works at Jones Spa. The manager asks, "Joan, will you report on the repair record of our computers?" Joan found that 14 of the 70 computers needed repair last year. Seven were in for repair for 3 weeks or longer. What portion of the computers needed repair last year?

   a. 1/5
   b. 3/7
   c. 1/2
   d. None of the above

8. Med Tech Supply has 300 products in inventory. The inventory manager needs to know how many products will bring in sales of $12,000 or more during the next year. Sales records for last year showed 1 of every 6 products had sales of $12,000 or more. Based on last year's records, what number should be provided to the inventory manager?

   a. 1/40
   b. $2,000
   c. 1/50
   d. 50

9. Thomas Dye is the exhibit manager for the Computer Trade Show. There are 144,000 square feet of exhibit space available, which will rent for $72,000. Byte Microcomputer Co. requested 1/24 of the total exhibit space if the cost does not exceed its budget of $3,000. Will the space rental fee exceed Byte's budget?

   a. Yes
   b. No

10. Brenda Cole is a partner in the law firm of Diaz, Cole, and Burns. Attorneys divide earnings based on their share of time spent on each case. A client was billed $4,800. Hours spent on the case by each attorney were as follows: Diaz, 6; Cole, 5; and Burns, 4. What was Cole's share of the billing?

    a. $4,800
    b. $960
    c. $14,400
    d. $1,600

11. Lisa Chang works at Ingrid's Interiors. A customer wants to purchase a $250 chair, which is reduced by 1/5 off its list price, and a $500 sofa, which is reduced by 1/4 off its price. How much will the customer be charged?

    a. $175

    b. $750

    c. $575

    d. $925

12. Danver Community College stocks Stylex Pens. The mail order catalog lists the pens at $7.20 for 12 pens. The college needs 360 pens. What will the pen order cost?

    a. $216

    b. $600

    c. $50

    d. None of the above

13. Gunter Mauer works at Melody Music Supply. Gunter received an order for 20 compact disks. The price is $12 each, plus $1.50 shipping charge per disk. What amount will the music store be billed for this order?

    a. $238.50

    b. $241.50

    c. $270

    d. None of the above

14. Maxine Patterson works at Desharzo and Hanna, Attorneys. A 4-week supply of covers for legal briefs is needed. The office uses about 30 covers per week. The covers cost $6.60 for 12, plus a $10 shipping charge from Direct Mail Plus. The Supply Shop sells covers for $.66 each with no shipping charge. Which supplier offers the best price?

    a. Direct Mail Plus

    b. The Supply Shop

15. Jacqueline Tucker works at Bright Eyes Makeup Co. The owner says, "Jacqueline, order 180 blush brushes, 70 boxes of cotton balls, and 6 boxes of concealer." Blush brushes sell for $.35 each, cotton balls for $.80 per box, and concealer for $14.95 per box. Shipping costs are $25. How much will the order cost?

   a. $233.70

   b. $208.70

   c. $183.70

   d. $289.70

16. Cecil Cranfield works for Cordova Imports. A customer was recently sent a bill for 150 items that each cost $55.50. Eight of the items were returned. The customer requested a $2.96 refund for the returned items. Is this the correct amount that Cecil should give as a refund?

   a. Yes

   b. No

17. Alan Jones works at Carson Electronics. Operating costs for the previous month were: salaries, $134,850; supplies, $21,000; and building and maintenance, $18,150. His supervisor, Anita Carlyle, asks, "Alan, what percent of the total operating cost is salaries?"

   a. 22.5 percent

   b. 77.5 percent

   c. 2.25 percent

   d. 7.75 percent

18. Jenny Bottoms works at Bank City. A customer says, "I want to open a savings account with a weekly deposit of at least $30. Will 6 percent of my $525 weekly salary allow me to deposit this much?" What should Jenny tell the customer?

   a. Yes, the amount will exceed $30.

   b. Yes, the amount is exactly $30.

   c. No, the amount is less than $30.

   d. More information is needed to compute the response.

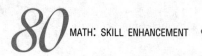

19. Bill Langston manages a branch office of Parasailing Plus. His annual salary is $42,000. Yesterday, Bill was asked to transfer to the home office location. If he agrees he will be awarded a 6.5 percent raise. What procedure should be used to compute the new salary?

   a. Multiply his annual salary by the raise percent.
   b. Multiply his annual salary by the raise percent. Then, add this amount to his annual salary.
   c. Multiply his annual salary by the raise percent. Then, subtract this amount from his annual salary.
   d. Divide his annual salary by the raise percent.

20. William Taylor is a salesperson. He is paid a commission on each sale. William recently made a $4,600 sale, which resulted in a $483 commission. What procedure is used to determine the commission percent?

   a. Divide the commission amount by the sales amount. Then, move the decimal point two places to the right in the answer.
   b. Divide the commission amount by the sales amount.
   c. Divide the sales amount by the commission amount. Then, move the decimal point two places to the right.
   d. The procedure depends on factors not provided in the problem.

21. Myra Quick works for Rent-a-Waterski. A billing clerk tells her, "According to my records, George Wagoner paid $400 on his account. This amount represents 5 percent of his balance due. Myra, what is the amount due for this account?"

   a. $400
   b. $800
   c. $2,000
   d. $8,000

22. The dean at Brackman College needs to know the ratio of students to faculty members at the college. A review of class records shows there are 20 faculty members and 1,600 students at the college. Each faculty member teaches 5 courses. What ratio should be reported to the dean?

   a. 5:1
   b. 20:1
   c. 80:1
   d. 1,600:1

23. Ray Schweitzer works at Export Management Center. Last week the manager said, "Ray, find the ratio of the number of employees to the number of employees absent last Monday. A ratio of 35 to 1 is acceptable." Ray found that 800 employees work for the firm; of the total, 25 were absent last Monday. Is the ratio acceptable?

    a. Yes

    b. No

24. Lisa Rasbach works at Smith Wholesalers, Inc. An employee ordered 40 boxes of metal clasps. The price was listed as 5 boxes for $3. What is the total cost of the 40 boxes of metal clasps that should be put on the order form?

    a. $120

    b. $15

    c. $24

    d. $66.67

25. Sandra Rush works at Brilliant Building Supply. A contractor asked Sandra to find the number of shingles needed for a new house with a roof measuring 5,400 square feet. It takes 30 packs of shingles to cover 3,000 square feet of roof. How many packs of shingles will be needed?

    a. 30 packs

    b. 54 packs

    c. 100 packs

    d. 180 packs

Answers: Quick Check and Explanations, see page 175.

Unit II Test

Read and solve the following problems. Write the letter of the correct answer on the answer sheet on page 211 at the end of the book. Only one answer is correct.

1. Debra Bale works at Rainbow Hot Air Balloons. The office manager said, "Our employees are absent from work too often. Of the 60 employees working in our office, 8 were absent last week. There were 15 employees absent the week before." What portion of the employees was absent last week? (Answer in a fraction.)

   a. 1/4
   b. 8/15
   c. 2/15
   d. 15/8

2. Amanda Cervani is assistant coach of a summer softball league for her company. The team coach says, "Amanda, of the 22 employees playing for the company team, 6 were absent from the last game and 8 were absent from the previous game." What portion of the team was absent from the last game? (Answer in a fraction.)

   a. 4/1
   b. 6/22
   c. 3/11
   d. 3/4

3. Quentin Esmano is an installation specialist for Tri-State Irrigation Systems. He often works evenings and on weekends during the summer months. He earned $21,000 regular pay and $7,000 overtime pay last year. What portion of his total pay was overtime pay? (Answer in a fraction.)

   a. 2/3
   b. 1/3
   c. 1/4
   d. None of the above

4. Ray Baker purchased a cabinet marked $696 and a sofa marked $840. However, both items were reduced by 25 percent during a special weekend sale. What amount should Ray pay for the two items?

   a. $384

   b. $1,152

   c. $1,920

   d. None of the above

5. Antonio Armandi is a receiving clerk for HICO Balloon Distributing. The accounting clerk says, "Antonio, we ordered 12,000 Valentine balloons. What portion of these balloons has been delivered to us so far?" Antonio found that 2,400 balloons arrived last week, and 4,800 arrived this week. What portion has arrived? (Answer in a fraction.)

   a. 6/10

   b. 1/5

   c. 2/5

   d. 3/5

6. There are three doctors at the QuickMed Emergency Center. Yesterday, Dr. Randon saw 9 patients, Dr. Munlawn saw 8, and Dr. Quinley saw 10. Each doctor's charges are based on his portion of the total patients seen each day. What portion of yesterday's patients did Dr. Randon see? (Answer in a fraction.)

   a. 1/3

   b. 2/3

   c. 9/27

   d. 2/5

7. Mary O'Neil visits the Downtown Furniture Center showroom with a $1,700 budget for furniture. She purchases 3 tables for $129.95 each and a bedroom suite for $1,299.95. Can Mary make this purchase and stay within her budget?

   a. Yes

   b. No

8. Baros, Gillman, and Wasmalor are partners in a home furnishings business. The partners agree to share profits based on the following investments: Baros, 1/4; Gillman, 1/2; and Wasmalor, 1/4. Last year, the business had a $88,000 profit. How much of the profit belongs to Baros?

    a. $44,000

    b. $22,000

    c. $66,000

    d. None of the above

9. Lily Maples administers a math test to her ninth-grade students. The test has 90 questions. In order to pass the test, the students must answer correctly at least 70 percent of the total questions. How many of the total questions must be answered correctly in order for a student to pass the test?

    a. 27

    b. 13

    c. 63

    d. 70

10. Tim Cowan works at Outdoor Sporting Goods. The owner says, "Tim, we use 17 memo pads per week. Please order enough pads for 5 weeks. Also order 70 computer disks." Memo pads sell for $.55 each, and computer disks sell for $14.95 per box. Each box contains 10 disks. Shipping costs will be $17. What will the order cost?

    a. $131

    b. $151.40

    c. $168.40

    d. $1,110.25

11. Simon Bagous, a part-time employee at Tan and Tone, is paid $9.20 per hour. A review of time cards showed that Simon worked 5 1/4 hours on Monday, 7 1/2 hours on Wednesday, and 4 3/4 hours on Friday. What amount did Simon earn for the week?

    a. $161.00

    b. $117.30

    c. $147.20

    d. None of the above

12. Alex Nardonti works for Pinson Coffee Shop. The owner asks Alex to research the cost of fire insurance premiums for the business. The owner wants the business to be insured for $230,000. Alex found the lowest rate available was $.00325 per dollar of insurance coverage. What is the premium amount at this rate?

    a. $7,475.00

    b. $747.50

    c. $74.75

    d. None of the above

13. Billy Joe Foster is a secretary in a law office. Part of his job is to maintain the office supplies. Attorneys and clients use about 75 legal pads per week. Legal pads cost $.84 for 12. How much will a 6-week supply of pads cost?

    a. $756

    b. $4,536

    c. $84

    d. $31.50

14. Save-the-Day Car Rental offers a compact car for a daily rental rate of $23.95 or a weekly rental rate of $128.00. Winston Levinson needs a compact car for only 5 days. Will the total rental fee for Winston be lower with the daily or the weekly rate?

    a. Daily

    b. Weekly

15. Sparkle Car Wash often runs special promotions to attract new customers. Fresh Scent Air Fresheners normally sell for $2.89 per package. During a promotion, the fresheners are offered at 3 packages for $7.00. Frank Coelho purchased 9 packages. What were his total savings?

    a. $8.67

    b. $21.00

    c. $26.01

    d. $5.01

16. Will Gottlieb wants to buy stock that costs $37.375 per share as an investment. He will invest $3,139.50 in this stock. How many shares of stock can he buy? (Round to even numbers, if necessary.)

    a. 84

    b. 177

    c. 3,102

    d. 8,400

17. Melissa and Amy Winslow decide to sell lemonade and cookies to earn money for summer camp. One family buys 4 cups of lemonade for $.40 each and 8 cookies for $.25 each. They pay with a $10.00 bill. How much change should the family get?

    a. $3.60

    b. $1.60

    c. $6.40

    d. $2.00

18. Ingrid Landler is an accounts receivable clerk for Dalton Glass Accessories. A customer was sent an invoice for 8 mirrored placemats totalling $263.60. The customer requested a refund for 2 of the placemats that were broken in shipment. What is the amount of the customer's refund?

    a. $65.90

    b. $32.95

    c. $16.00

    d. $43.93

19. Jim Johnson works at Allforms Printing. Last month operating expenses included salaries, $135,200; supplies, $14,365; and building and maintenance, $19,435. Jim's supervisor asked him what percent of the total expenses was spent on salaries. What percent should Jim answer?

    a. 8 percent

    b. 80 percent

    c. 10.6 percent

    d. 14.3 percent

20. Cynthia Guessman works at Hanson Medical Clinic. The doctor says, "Cindy, what percent of our overdue patient accounts are more than 90 days overdue?" Cindy found the following: Total of accounts 30 days or less overdue, $4,620; accounts more than 30 days but less than 90 days overdue, $3,360; and accounts 90 days or more overdue, $2,520. What percent should Cindy report to Dr. Hanson?

   a. 44 percent
   b. 24 percent
   c. 32 percent
   d. None of the above

21. Brandon Jernigan works at Fisher Floor Fashions. Total expenses for the previous month were $246,000. Of this amount, $127,920 related to salaries. Brandon was asked to compute the percent of expenses the business spent on salaries. What percent should Brandon report?

   a. .52 percent
   b. 48 percent
   c. 5.2 percent
   d. 52 percent

22. Pamela Hollis is a systems analyst with Goodspot Hotels. Her annual salary is $48,000. Pamela was offered a chance to transfer to New York and receive a 6 percent raise. A competing hotel chain in Chicago offered her a job with a $50,000 annual salary. Which location offered the highest salary?

   a. New York
   b. Chicago

23. Delana Cantrell is a sales clerk at Yogurt Cone Castle. Her annual salary is $17,820. She receives an equal portion of her salary each month. Delana is offered a promotion to assistant manager with a 9 percent raise. What is the dollar amount of Delana's raise on a monthly basis?

   a. $1,485.00
   b. $133.65
   c. $148.50
   d. $160.38

24. Ed Carney works at a small insurance agency. The president asked Ed to find the ratio of employees over 55 years old to total employees. Ed found 14 employees were over 55 years old. The remaining 28 employees were under 55 years old. What is the ratio of employees over 55 years old to total employees?

    a. 1:2
    b. 1:3
    c. 1:55
    d. 1:28

25. Brad Phillips works at Carpenter Electronics, which makes electronic circuits for computers. His supervisor says, "Brad, we make 3,600 circuits during our two shifts—16 hours. How many circuits will we produce if each shift is expanded 2 hours for a total of 20 hours?"

    a. 1,800
    b. 5,400
    c. 4,500
    d. 72,000

CALCULATING UNITS OF MEASURE

T he first five problems that follow are warmup exercises to give you a chance to practice basic math skills. You may use a calculator or paper and pencil. Circle the letter of the correct answer, and compare your answers with those on page 180. If your answers are correct, go on to complete the problems in this section. If the answers you select are incorrect, try the problems again. If you continue to answer the questions incorrectly, see your instructor before attempting to complete this section.

The following conversion factors will be useful for this section:

60 seconds	=	1 minute
60 minutes	=	1 hour
24 hours	=	1 day
7 days	=	1 week
365 days	=	1 year
52 weeks	=	1 year
12 months	=	1 year

1. Change to hours: 210 minutes = ?

   a. 21 hours

   b. 3.5 hours

   c. 3 hours

   d. 2.5 hours

2. Determine the hours: 9:15 a.m. to 2:45 p.m. = ?

    a. 11 hours
    b. 5 hours
    c. 5 1/4 hours
    d. 5 1/2 hours

3. Add: 5 hours, 45 minutes + 6 hours, 38 minutes = ?

    a. 11 hours, 23 minutes
    b. 12 hours, 23 minutes
    c. 12 hours, 32 minutes
    d. 12 hours, 53 minutes

4. Determine the years: 72 months = ?

    a. 7 years
    b. 6.5 years
    c. 6 years
    d. 5.5 years

5. Determine the weeks: 3.5 years = ?

    a. 182 weeks
    b. 178 weeks
    c. 172 weeks
    d. 156 weeks

Read and solve the following problems. You will need to decide which basic math calculations are needed to solve each problem. Circle the letter of the correct answer from the choices offered. Only one answer is correct. Then compare your answers with those starting on page 180. When you select an incorrect answer, information will be given to help you learn how to solve the problem.

6. Debbie West is a court reporter. Debbie's time card for last week shows 5 hours, 30 minutes on Monday and 6 hours, 45 minutes on Tuesday. How many total hours did Debbie work last week?

    a. 11 hours
    b. 1 1/4 hours
    d. 12 hours
    d. 12 1/4 hours

7. Ron Smith divides his time between two branch offices of City Office Supply. Last week Ron spent 5 hours, 45 minutes on Tuesday and 7 hours, 45 minutes on Thursday at the midtown branch. How many total hours did Ron spend at this location?

   a. 2 hours
   b. 12 1/2 hours
   c. 13 1/2 hours
   d. 12 hours

8. Marilyn Duncan took the bar exam in preparation to become an attorney. She was 1 of 3 applicants taking the test on November 15. The results will be ready in 6 weeks. How many days will she have to wait for the results?

   a. 2
   b. 18
   c. 42
   d. 90

9. Sharon Wells installs computer networks. She charges clients based on the amount of time spent on a job. She spent 6 3/4 hours on Monday and 5 1/2 hours on Wednesday installing a network at Medco. How many hours should she bill Medco for the installation?

   a. 12 1/2 hours
   b. 12 1/4 hours
   c. 11 hours
   d. 1 1/4 hours

10. Dan Toro, a repairman at All Season Appliances, serviced the air conditioning unit at Beckman Labs on Monday and Tuesday. He spent 8 1/4 hours on Monday and 9 1/2 hours on Tuesday. How many hours should Beckman Labs be billed for the job?

    a. 17 3/4 hours
    b. 17 1/4 hours
    c. 17 hours
    d. 3/4 hours

11. The Wild Blue Flying Service provides airplane flying lessons. Bess Bonera had lessons for 3 1/4 hours on Monday, 2 1/2 hours on Wednesday, and 2 3/4 hours on Friday. How many hours will Wild Blue charge Bess?

    a. 7 hours

    b. 7 3/4 hours

    c. 8 1/2 hours

    d. 8 3/4 hours

12. Tom Pittman earns $8 per hour working part-time for Classic Furniture Center. He must work at least 15 hours per week. Tom worked 6 1/2 hours on Thursday, 5 3/4 hours on Friday, and 8 hours on Saturday. How many hours should Tom be paid for?

    a. 19 hours

    b. 20 1/4 hours

    c. 20 1/2 hours

    d. 35 1/4 hours

13. Kiko Kokonoe is a trainee for City Center Computer Sales. The company offered Kiko a choice of $1,500 monthly salary plus a $500 bonus at the end of the year or a $300 weekly salary. Which salary plan gives the highest pay?

    a. Monthly plan

    b. Weekly plan

14. Mary Kate Romeno is a payroll clerk for Murphy Builders. Thomas O'Connor, a carpenter, worked 8 hours each day (Monday through Friday) last week except Tuesday, when he left 3 hours, 30 minutes early. How many work hours should Mary Kate record for the week?

    a. 40 hours

    b. 43 1/2 hours

    c. 37 hours

    d. 36 1/2 hours

15. Sandra Goldman, a construction worker for Longview Construction Company, worked 8 hours each of the 5 working days (Monday through Friday) last week and 3 3/4 hours on Saturday. How many total hours did Sandra work?

    a. 43 3/4 hours
    b. 40 hours
    c. 43 hours
    d. 36 1/4 hours

16. Martin Macias fills out employee time cards at A-1 Home Builders. Ted Carlson, a bricklayer, began work at 8 A.M. and left work at 11:30 A.M. on Monday. On Tuesday, he began work at 7:30 A.M. and left work at 11:15 A.M. How many hours should Martin enter for Ted during this time period?

    a. 7 hours
    b. 7 1/4 hours
    c. 7 1/2 hours
    d. 7 3/4 hours

17. Counter Workers at Harris Deli normally work 5 days per week from 8 A.M. to 5 P.M., with an hour off for lunch without pay. Nancy Boyd worked until 5:30 P.M. on Tuesday and clocked out at 3:15 P.M. on Friday. The other three days were normal. How many hours did Nancy work during this time period?

    a. 40 hours
    b. 40 1/2 hours
    c. 38 1/4 hours
    d. 38 3/4 hours

18. The Drexel Corporation decided to award a trophy to the employee with the fastest keyboarding speed in the company. Randy Hall had an average keyboarding speed of 180 characters per minute for 1 hour. Bernie Smith keyed 10,000 characters during the hour. Which employee should receive the award?

    a. Randy Hall
    b. Bernie Smith

19. Bertha Jefferson gives exams to applicants for data entry jobs. This 6-part, 1 1/2-hour exam requires an equal amount of time for each part. Bertha times each part separately. How much time does she allow for each part?

   a. 15 minutes

   b. 60 minutes

   c. 90 minutes

   d. None of the above

20. Tracy Hildebrand bought a new car at Downtown Auto. She will pay for the car over a 42-month period. How many years will Tracy be paying for the car under this plan?

   a. 4 years

   b. 3 1/2 years

   c. 12 years

   d. 3 years

21. Goode Motor Sales provides several payment options for customers: Plan A: $100 per week for 3 years; Plan B: $425 per month for 3 years; Plan C: $200 every two weeks for 3 years; or Plan D: $900 every 2 months for 3 years. Which plan will result in the highest total cost?

   a. Plan A

   b. Plan B

   c. Plan C

   d. Plan D

22. Ray Rodriquez will be eligible for retirement benefits in 72 months. How many years remain before Ray can retire?

   a. 7.2 years

   b. 6 1/2 years

   c. 6 years

   d. None of the above

23. Bob Schultz is a part-time office clerk at Kyoto Savings & Loan. Bob attends high school and is limited by law from working more than 27 hours per week. He worked 5 hours, 30 minutes on Monday; 6 hours, 45 minutes on Wednesday; 7 hours, 45 minutes on Friday; and 8 hours on Saturday. Did his work time exceed the legal limit?

   a. Yes

   b. No

24. Patel Furniture Center allows customers to buy furniture and pay for it in 60 days with no finance charge. A customer purchased furniture on October 23. What is the last date that payment can be made without the finance charge?

    a. December 22
    b. December 23
    c. December 24
    d. December 25

25. Nancy Glassick is scheduled to begin her first day on the production line at Fresh Skateboard Manufacturing. Nancy will be given 3 weeks vacation each year and required to work the remaining weeks. How many weeks will she need to work each year?

    a. 3
    b. 17
    c. 49
    d. 55

Answers: Quick check and Explanations, see page 180.

Length

The first five problems that follow are warmup exercises to give you a chance to practice basic math skills. You may use a calculator or paper and pencil. Circle the letter of the correct answer, and compare your answers with those on page 185. If your answers are correct, go on to complete the problems in this section. If the answers you select are incorrect, try the problems again. If you continue to answer the questions incorrectly, see your instructor before attempting to complete this section.

The following conversion factors will be useful for this section:

12 inches	=	1 foot
36 inches	=	1 yard
3 feet	=	1 yard
5280 feet	=	1 mile
1760 yards	=	1 mile

1. Change 72 inches to feet:
   a. 12 feet
   b. 7 feet
   c. 6 feet
   d. 2 feet

2. Add: 8 feet, 7 inches + 9 feet, 10 inches = ?

   a. 17 feet, 3 inches
   b. 18 feet, 7 inches
   c. 18 feet, 5 inches
   d. 18 feet, 4 inches

3. Subtract: 5 yards, 1 foot − 2 yards, 2 feet = ?

   a. 3 yards, 1 foot
   b. 2 yards, 1 foot
   c. 2 yards, 2 feet
   d. 2 yards, 1 foot

4. Add: 4 yards, 2 feet + 2 yards, 2 feet = ?

   a. 7 yards, 2 feet
   b. 7 yards, 1 foot
   c. 7 yards
   d. 2 yards

5. Change 1.5 miles to feet.

   a. 18 feet
   b. 5,280 feet
   c. 7,920 feet
   d. 8,920 feet

Read and solve the following problems. You will need to decide which basic math calculations are needed to solve each problem. Circle the letter of the correct answer from the choices offered. Only one answer is correct. Then compare your answers with those starting on page 185. When you select an incorrect answer, information will be given to help you learn how to solve the problem.

6. The Thorsberg Corporation is installing computers on each employee's desk. The desks are 6 feet wide. Each computer requires 26 inches. The telephone requires an additional 9 inches and at least 36 additional inches must be available for books and other supplies. Is there enough space for the complete system?

   a. Yes
   b. No

7. The office manager at Modern Graphics needs to put bookcases across one wall of an office measuring 7 feet, 6 inches. How many 30-inch wide bookcases will fit on that side of the room?

   a. 2

   b. 3

   c. 4

   d. None of the above

8. Dietz and Yen, Tax Preparers, installed modems in two computers. One installation required 23 feet of phone cable. The other required 40 feet. The installer brought 20 yards of cable. Will this cable be enough to do the job?

   a. Yes

   b. No

9. The Connection Company installed cables to connect two networks. The first network is in Room 1217. The second network is in Room 1245, 48 feet from Room 1217. Cables to connect the networks are sold only by the yard. How many yards were required to do the job?

   a. 3

   b. 16

   c. 144

   d. 51

10. Dominica Fazio works in a warehouse. She needs to put 15 boxes on a shelf in the warehouse that measures 5 yards, 2 feet. Each box measures 27 inches long. Will these boxes fit on the shelf?

    a. Yes

    b. No

11. Barbara Rieves is a graphics design artist at Tronix Corporation. One of her assignments is to design an advertising brochure. Typeset material for a brochure uses 12 spaces per inch of type. How many spaces will fit on a page that is 9 1/2 inches wide?

    a. 21 1/2

    b. 2 1/2

    c. 108

    d. 114

12. City Office Supply sold a desk to the Design Print Shop. Design's office door measured 41 inches wide. The desk was 3 feet, 4 inches wide. Did the desk fit through the door?

  a. Yes

  b. No

  c. More measurements are needed

  d. Depends on the moving company

13. The Pennypincher Company tries to save money. They decide to re-ink their 140-inch printer ribbons. The Inkwell Ribbon Inker can fit ribbons up to 12 feet long. Will the inker work for Pennypincher's ribbons?

  a. Yes

  b. No

14. The Hobson Company decided to provide uniforms for each of the 6 members of the office support staff. One uniform requires 4 2/3 yards of material. The material can be bought in only one size—30 yards per bolt of cloth. Will one bolt of cloth be enough to make the uniforms?

  a. Yes

  b. No

15. Sherri Holtz works at DiBernardo Tile Company. The supervisor calls the office and says, "I need enough linoleum to cover a floor that is 1,248 square feet. Please order enough to do the job." Sherri finds that each roll of linoleum covers 32 square feet. How many rolls should Sherri order?

  a. 32

  b. 39

  c. 1,216

  d. 1,280

16. Diane Clearwater is the Smith Company office manager. The president of Smith Company saw a rug at a rug gallery that he liked. He asked Diane to see if it would fit in his office. The office measures 15 feet by 12 feet. The rug measured 4 yards by 2 yards. Did the rug fit?

  a. Yes

  b. No

17. The perimeter of a hallway in an office building measured 165 feet. The building manager ordered a wallpaper border for the perimeter of the hallway. A border that measures 59 yards is available at a local interior design store. Is this sufficient for the hallway?

    a. Yes
    b. No

18. George Chang connects computers to networks. He needs to connect 36 computers to a network. Each one will require 45 inches of cable. George has 40 yards of cable on his truck. Will this be enough to cable the network?

    a. Yes
    b. No

19. Jon Melchiori owns a company that cables communications equipment in offices. He purchased 3 rolls of cable. Each roll has 24 yards of cable. How many feet of cable did Jon purchase?

    a. 216
    b. 72
    c. 24
    d. None of the above

20. The Facemate Corporation has two offices 4.4 miles apart. The director of telecommunications decided to link these two offices by connecting them with a fiber optic cable. How many feet of cable is needed to connect the two offices?

    a. 5,280 feet
    b. 1,200 feet
    c. 23,232 feet
    d. None of the above

21. The Facemate Corporation decided to use fiber optic cables to connect the main office with a site 0.6 miles away. The building contractor estimated that approximately 4,000 feet of fiber optic cabling would be needed. Is this enough cable?

    a. Yes
    b. No

22. The Cisco Cookie Company decided to build a fence around their parking lot. The distance around the lot is 0.4 miles. Ace Fence Company agreed to do the job for $6,500. Reliable Fence Company agreed to do the job for $3 per foot. Which company offers the lowest amount?

    a. Ace Fence Company
    b. Reliable Fence Company

23. Mercury Irrigation Systems installs automatic sprinkler systems. A local university requested a bid to lay 2,400 yards of irrigation pipe. Mercury bid $4 per yard. A second company, Outdoor Systems, bid $1.50 per foot for the same job. Which bid is lower?

    a. Mercury Irrigation Systems
    b. Outdoor Systems

24. Each year Dunsmore Day Care Center puts a string of holiday lights around its two buildings. One building requires 12 yards, 2 feet, and 9 inches of lights. The second building requires 38 yards, 1 foot, and 8 inches of wire. The Center has 200 feet of lights. Will this be enough?

    a. Yes
    b. No

25. The City of Youngstown placed Christmas lights along the city streets, a distance of 5.8 miles. One company bid $18,000 for the job. A second company bid $.50 per foot for the job. A third company bid $1 per yard for the job. Which bid is lowest?

    a. First company
    b. Second company
    c. Third company
    d. Lowest bid cannot be determined

Answers: Quick Check and Explanations, see page 185.

Weight 12

The first five problems that follow are warmup exercises to give you a chance to practice basic math skills. You may use a calculator or paper and pencil. Circle the letter of the correct answer, and compare your answers with those on page 189. If your answers are correct, go on to complete the problems in this section. If the answers you select are incorrect, try the problems again. If you continue to answer the questions incorrectly, see your instructor before attempting to complete this section.

The following conversion factors will be useful for this section:

> 16 ounces = 1 pound
>
> 2,000 pounds = 1 ton

1. Change to pounds: 24 ounces = ?

   a. 24 pounds

   b. 16 pounds

   c. 2.4 pounds

   d. 1.5 pounds

2. Add: 10 pounds, 12 ounces + 8 pounds, 7 ounces = ?

   a. 19 pounds, 6 ounces

   b. 19 pounds, 3 ounces

   c. 19 pounds, 1 ounce

   d. 19 pounds

3. Multiply: 4 pounds, 6 ounces x 12 = ?

   a. 48 pounds

   b. 48 pounds, 12 ounces

   c. 52 pounds, 8 ounces

   d. 53 pounds, 8 ounces

4. Subtract: 8 pounds, 7 ounces – 2 pounds, 10 ounces = ?

   a. 6 pounds, 3 ounces

   b. 6 pounds, 1 ounces

   c. 5 pounds, 14 ounces

   d. 5 pounds, 13 ounces

5. Multiply and change to tons: 200 pounds x 30 = ?

   a. 60 tons

   b. 36 tons

   c. 6 tons

   d. 3 tons

Read and solve the following problems. You will need to decide which basic math calculations are needed to solve each problem. Circle the letter of the correct answer from the choices offered. Only one answer is correct. Then compare your answers with those starting on page 189. When you select an incorrect answer, information will be given to help you learn how to solve the problem.

6. Microcomputers Unlimited ships computers to mail order customers across the country. Shipping charges are added to the cost of the computer. What is the most likely unit of weight that will be used for a single computer?

   a. Ounces

   b. Pounds

   c. Tons

   d. None of the above

7. What is the best procedure to convert weight from ounces to pounds?

   a. Divide the number of ounces by 16 to represent the number of pounds. The remainder represents the number of ounces remaining.

   b. Multiply the number of ounces by 16.

   c. Add 16 to the number of ounces.

   d. Subtract 16 from the number of ounces.

8. Video Now ships videotapes to customers by overnight delivery. Each tape weighs 4 ounces. What is the weight of 20 tapes?

   a. 24 pounds
   b. 5 ounces
   c. 80 ounces
   d. 5 pounds

9. The Copier Manufacturing Company shipped a copier weighing 10 pounds, 15 ounces. The shipping container for the copier weighed 1 pound, 3 ounces. What was the total weight of the shipment?

   a. 12 pounds, 2 ounces
   b. 9 pounds, 12 ounces
   c. 20 pounds, 30 ounces
   d. None of the above

10. Miracle Marketing shipped two packages. One package weighed 4 pounds, 14 ounces. The other package weighed 2 pounds, 7 ounces. What was the total weight of the two packages?

    a. 2 pounds, 2 ounces
    b. 2 pounds, 7 ounces
    c. 7 pounds, 5 ounces
    d. None of the above

11. International Office Machines shipped 25 pieces of office equipment. Each piece weighed approximately 5 pounds, 8 ounces. The freight company agreed to charge for a shipment with a total weight of 127 pounds or actual weight if less than 127 pounds. Which is the lower weight?

    a. Approximate weight of 5 pounds, 8 ounces each piece
    b. Agreed total weight of 127 pounds

12. Holly Stores purchased 8 reams of paper for a laser printer. The total weight of the paper was 16 pounds, 8 ounces. What was the weight of each ream?

    a. 8 pounds, 4 ounces
    b. 2 pounds, 1 ounce
    c. 132 pounds
    d. 24 pounds

13. Lawhorn Company prepared 8 items for a shipment with a total weight of 4 pounds, 5 ounces. One item weighing 12 ounces was lost. What was the weight of the remaining items in the shipment?

    a. 34 pounds, 8 ounces

    b. 3 pounds, 9 ounces

    c. 5 pounds, 1 ounce

    d. None of the above.

14. A shipping carton has the strength to hold up to 10 pounds. An order is received for 6 office machines, each weighing 1 pound, 8 ounces. Is the shipping carton strong enough to handle the complete order?

    a. Yes

    b. No

15. Four employees work in the order department. An order is placed for 200 items, each one weighing 1 pound, 8 ounces. In order to find the total weight of the order, what information given above is not needed to solve the problem?

    a. Number of items

    b. Weight per item

    c. Number of employees

    d. Number of items and weight per item

16. Four employees work in the shipping department. They usually work 8 hours per day. An order is placed for 200 items, each one weighing 1 pound, 8 ounces. In order to find the total weight of the order, what information *is* needed to solve the problem?

    a. Number of items only

    b. Number of items and weight per item

    c. Number of employees and hours worked per day

    d. Number of employees and weight per item

17. Four employees work in the shipping department. They normally work 8 hours per day. An order is placed for 200 items, each one weighing 1 pound, 8 ounces. The total weight of the order is required to compute shipping charges. What is the total weight of the order?

    a. 1,600 pounds

    b. 200 pounds

    c. 300 pounds

    d. 201 pounds, 8 ounces

18. A laptop computer with carrying case weighs 22 pounds, 5 ounces. The case weighs 15 ounces. What is the weight of the computer without the case?

    a. 23 pounds, 4 ounces

    b. 21 pounds, 6 ounces

    c. 22 pounds, 5 ounces

    d. None of the above

19. Daily Data Services printed 100 directories for a company. Each directory weighed 1 pound, 8 ounces. Quick Freight Company agreed to ship them for $1.00 per pound. Express Today agreed to ship them for $207 total. Which carrier offered the lowest price for shipping?

    a. Quick Freight Company

    b. Express Today

20. Daily Data Services printed 200 directories weighing 3 pounds, 8 ounces each. Quick Freight Company agreed to ship the items for $.50 per pound. Express Today agreed to ship the entire order for $307. National Express agreed to ship the items for $1.50 per item. Which carrier offered the lowest price?

    a. Quick Freight Company

    b. Express Today

    c. National Express

21. Rose Publishing needs to ship 300 books to California. Each book weighs 1 pound, 4 ounces. Each shipping envelope has the strength to hold up to 5 pounds. The stock clerk finds 90 envelopes in inventory. Will this supply be sufficient for the order?

    a. Yes

    b. No

22. The Fancy Chocolate Factory received a shipment of chocolate bars. Each bar weighed 1 pound, 8 ounces. The total order weighed 375 pounds. The store manager says, "Estimate the number of bars received. We ordered 248 bars, but will count them later." Was the estimate reasonably close to the number ordered?

    a. Yes

    b. No

23. Gallini Freight Lines often uses trucks to deliver packages to local customers. On one order, 300 packages weighing 20 pounds each are loaded on the truck. What is the weight of the load?

    a. 15 tons
    b. 3 tons
    c. 6,000 tons
    d. None of the above

24. Ready Mix sells asphalt paving for roads. The company charges for the asphalt by the ton. Truck #12 had 7,000 pounds of asphalt. Truck #23 had 5,000 pounds of asphalt. What was the combined weight in tons of asphalt on the two trucks?

    a. 12 tons
    b. 12,000 tons
    c. 6 tons
    d. None of the above

25. Ready Mix's trucks can carry a maximum of 7,000 pounds of asphalt mix. The production manager asks Carmen Shapiro, an office clerk, "Carmen, we have made 14 deliveries of asphalt for the Cook Road Project. How many tons of asphalt have we delivered for this project?"

    a. 98 tons
    b. 500 tons
    c. 49 tons
    d. None of the above

Answers: Quick Check and Explanations, see page 189.

Combination Problems

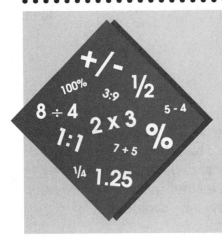

The first five problems that follow are warmup exercises to give you a chance to practice basic math skills. You may use a calculator or paper and pencil. Circle the letter of the correct answer, and compare your answers with those on page 195. If your answers are correct, go on to complete the problems in this section. If the answers you select are incorrect, try the problems again. If you continue to answer the questions incorrectly, see your instructor before attempting to complete this section.

1. Add: 4 hours, 25 minutes + 8 hours, 50 minutes = ?

   a. 11 hours, 15 minutes

   b. 12 hours, 55 minutes

   c. 13 hours, 15 minutes

   d. 13 hours, 25 minutes

2. Multiply: 24 hours x 4 1/2 = ?

   a. 96.5 hours

   b. 98 hours

   c. 106 hours

   d. 108 hours

3. Subtract: 30 yards − 5 yards, 2 feet = ?

   a. 25 yards

   b. 24 yards, 1 foot

   c. 24 yards, 2 feet

   d. 23 yards, 1 foot

4. Change 69 feet to yards.

   a. 23 yards

   b. 9 yards

   c. 6 yards

   d. 3 yards

5. Add: 4 pounds, 12 ounces + 8 pounds, 10 ounces = ?

   a. 12 pounds, 6 ounces

   b. 13 pounds, 6 ounces

   c. 13 pounds, 5 ounces

   d. 13 pounds, 4 ounces

Read and solve the following problems. You will need to decide which basic math calculations are needed to solve each problem. Circle the letter of the correct answer from the choices offered. Only one answer is correct. Then compare your answers with those starting on page 195. When you select an incorrect answer, information will be given to help you learn how to solve the problem.

6. Jim Takahashi earns $8.25 per hour working part-time in the law offices of Benz and Taylor. Last week he worked 5 1/4 hours on Monday, 6 1/2 hours on Wednesday, and 4 3/4 hours on Friday. How many hours did Jim work last week?

   a. 15

   b. 8.25

   c. 16 1/2

   d. 17 1/2

7. Jim DeSica is a consultant for a local landscape firm. He bills clients for time spent on projects. A job at Benzinger Corp. required 5 1/2 hours planning, 6 1/4 hours drawing the landscape plan, and 3 1/2 hours showing the design to the company. How many hours will Jim bill for the project?

   a. 14

   b. 15

   c. 15 1/4

   d. None of the above

8. Les Slough is a court reporter. He records trials and then transcribes his notes. A recent trial lasted 4 hours and 45 minutes on Monday and 5 hours and 30 minutes on Tuesday. The time required to transcribe the notes was 6 hours and 45 minutes. How much time should Les bill for his services?

   a. 15 hours

   b. 3 hours, 30 minutes

   c. 17 hours

   d. None of the above

9. Cristina Burke owns a company that does word processing for local businesses. She estimated a recent job would require 15 hours. Actual time spent on the job was 4 hours on Monday, 6 hours and 45 minutes on Tuesday, and 3 hours and 30 minutes on Wednesday. Was she able to complete the job within the estimated time period?

   a. Yes

   b. No

10. Glynda Luttman is a payroll clerk for Distinctive Builders. Will Brown, a construction worker, normally works 8 hours each day, Monday through Friday. However, he left work 4 hours and 15 minutes early on Thursday. How many hours did Mr. Brown work last week?

    a. 40

    b. 44 1/4

    c. 36 3/4

    d. 35 3/4

11. Danny Romero maintains time cards for City Office Supply. Employees usually work from 8 A.M. to 5 P.M. each day, with an hour off for lunch without pay. However, Daryl Jones worked until 5:45 P.M. on Monday and clocked out at 3:30 P.M. on Wednesday. Other days he worked the regular hours. How many hours should Danny record for Daryl Jones?

    a. 39 1/4

    b. 42 1/4

    c. 40

    d. None of the above

12. Jose Angulo is eligible for an auto loan that requires a $349 monthly payment for 54 months. How many years would Jose have to repay the loan?

   a. 349

   b. 4

   c. 12

   d. 4 1/2

13. Alex Bassi is a new employee at Hasty Print. During his employment interview, he was told that he would be given 4 weeks vacation each year. How many weeks will Alex be required to work during the year?

   a. 4

   b. 13

   c. 48

   d. 56

14. Felicia Ferrari takes college classes and works part-time. The work-study program limits students work to a maximum of 25 hours per week. Felicia worked 5 3/4 hours on Monday, 6 1/2 hours on Tuesday, 8 hours on Wednesday, and 4 3/4 hours on Friday. Did Felicia exceed the limit?

   a. Yes

   b. No

15. Ingrid's Interiors decided to install computers in two offices. One office will require 34 feet of printer cable. The other office will require 29 feet of printer cable. The printer installer has 20 yards of cable. Is this enough cable?

   a. Yes

   b. No

16. Roadmap Trucking needs to connect two networks that are 54 feet apart. How many yards of cable will be required to do the job?

   a. 54

   b. 51

   c. 18

   d. 162

17. Timely Trucking decided that 5 office employees should wear uniforms to work. One uniform will require 5 4/5 yards of material. The material chosen can only be purchased in one size—30 yards per bolt of cloth. Will one bolt of cloth be enough to make the uniforms?

   a. Yes
   b. No

18. Sue Fongu is purchasing assistant at a local construction firm. One of the jobs requires roofing a 23,464 square foot building. One sheet of plywood covers 28 square feet. How many plywood sheets should Sue purchase for the job?

   a. 838
   b. 656,992
   c. 23,436
   d. 23,492

19. Home Property Management decided to obtain two cost estimates to build a fence around one of their properties—a distance of 0.5 miles. Ole Town Fence Co. bid $9,000 for the job. Tri-State Fence Co. agreed to do the job for $4 per foot. Which offer was lowest?

   a. Ole Town Fence Co.
   b. Tri-State Fence Co.

20. Homestead Properties decided to install an automatic sprinkler system on their lot. About 1,500 feet of pipe will be required for the job. City Systems made a bid to do the job for $4 per yard. Nature Systems made a bid to do the job for $2,100. Which bid was lowest?

   a. City Systems
   b. Nature Systems

21. Council Laketown decided to install decorations on 6.5 miles of city streets in honor of its one hundredth birthday. They decided to budget $25,000 for the project. Outdoors Unlimited bid $.60 per foot for the job. Nature Center bid $1.50 per yard for the job. Which bid should be accepted?

   a. Outdoors Unlimited
   b. Nature Center
   c. None—both bids are over the budget
   d. Not enough data is provided

22. Leslie Black is a mail clerk at Howard Corp. One of the departments shipped 10 portable radios weighing 14 ounces each. What is the total weight of this shipment?

    a. 10 pounds
    b. 14 pounds
    c. 8 3/4 pounds
    d. 2,240 pounds

23. Olivia Puente purchased 24 reams of laser printer paper with a total weight of 72 pounds. What is the weight of each ream of printer paper?

    a. 72 pounds
    b. 3 pounds
    c. 1,728 pounds
    d. 96 pounds

24. A shipping carton has the strength to hold up to 24 pounds. An order is received for 18 calculators, each one weighing 1 pound and 2 ounces. Is the shipping carton strong enough to handle the shipment?

    a. Yes
    b. No

25. Timely Trucking charges customers based on the distance shipped and weight of the shipment. A local customer shipped an order to a nearby city. Each of the 350 packages weighed 80 pounds. What is the total weight of the shipment?

    a. 14 tons
    b. 4.375 tons
    c. 2,000 tons
    d. None of the above

Answers: Quick Check and Explanations, see page 195.

Unit III Test

Read and solve the following problems. Write the letter of the correct answer on the answer sheet on page 213 at the end of the book. Only one answer is correct.

1. Marta Gonzalez is a service technician for a computer repair service. She charges clients by the hour. She worked at City Services for 4 3/4 hours on Monday, 3 1/2 hours on Wednesday, and 5 3/4 hours on Thursday. How many hours should Marta bill City Services?

   a. 12 hours
   b. 13 hours
   c. 14 hours
   d. 15 hours

2. Eva Washburn is a court reporter for a Minneapolis firm. Eva's time card shows 4 hours, 45 minutes on Tuesday and 5 hours, 30 minutes on Wednesday. How many total hours did Eva work this week?

   a. 9 hours, 30 minutes
   b. 10 hours
   c. 10 hours, 15 minutes
   d. 9 hours, 45 minutes

3. Laban Connelly will be arriving in Japan on June 15 to secure a contract for a distributorship. He will be based in Japan for 8 weeks. How many total days will he be in Japan?

   a. 49
   b. 56
   c. 64
   d. 15

4. Juan Gomez is a repairman at A-1 Television. He usually works from 8 A.M. to 5 P.M. 5 days a week. He takes an hour off for lunch without pay. Juan clocked out at 2:15 P.M. on Wednesday and at 3:30 P.M. on Friday. He worked his normal hours the rest of the week. How many hours did Juan work during the week?

   a. 44 1/4 hours

   b. 40 hours

   c. 35 3/4 hours

   d. 8 hours

5. Matilda Hisbon maintains time cards at Smiley Dan's Auto Dealership. Christina Tomlinson, a part-time employee, worked two days last week. She began work at 8:30 A.M. and left work at 1:30 P.M. on Monday. On Tuesday, she began work at 9:00 A.M. and left work at 4:30 P.M. How many hours should Matilda compute for Christina during this time period?

   a. 12 1/2 hours

   b. 13 hours

   c. 14 1/2 hours

   d. 13 1/2 hours

6. Shane Raulerson signed a 30-month contract to lease an automobile. How many years will Shane have the car leased?

   a. 3 years

   b. 3 1/2 years

   c. 2 1/2 years

   d. 4 years

7. Bill Smith, a construction worker, usually works 8 hours during each of 5 days (Monday through Friday). Last week, he became ill on Tuesday and left work 2 hours and 30 minutes early. He worked from 8 A.M. to 9:45 A.M. on Saturday. He worked his normal hours the rest of the week. How many hours did Bill work last week?

   a. 39 hours

   b. 39 1/4 hours

   c. 37 1/2 hours

   d. 35 3/4 hours

8. Reddington Junior College will be installing cables to connect a local area network between two offices. The offices are located 57 feet apart. How many yards will be required to do the job?

   a. 144 yards
   b. 19 yards
   c. 28 1/2 yards
   d. 171 yards

9. One fabric window treatment for the reception area in Dr. Daniel Vecera's office requires 8 1/8 yards of fabric. The office has 4 windows needing this same treatment. How many total yards of fabric will be required for the 4 window treatments?

   a. 35 yards
   b. 34 1/2 yards
   c. 32 1/8 yards
   d. 32 1/2 yards

10. Sarah Goodrum bought a used car from City Auto. She could choose from four payment plans: a) $125 per week for 3 years; b) $525 per month for 3 years; c) $220 every two weeks for 3 years; or d) $500 every month for 3 years. Which plan will result in the lowest total cost to Sarah?

    a. Plan A
    b. Plan B
    c. Plan C
    d. Plan D

11. Astrid Himer works for Coney Construction Company. The roofing supervisor calls the office and says, "I am on site #5839 and need enough plywood to cover a roof that is 1,440 square feet. Please send enough plywood for this job." Astrid knows that each plywood sheet covers 32 square feet. How many plywood sheets should Astrid send to the site?

    a. 42
    b. 32
    c. 45
    d. 144

12. Sidney Rice is a network specialist. He is responsible for running cable for a computer laboratory with 28 computers. Each computer requires 60 inches of cabling. Sidney has 45 yards of cabling on his truck. Will this amount of cable be sufficient to cable the network?

a. Yes

b. No

13. Tom D'Avila received a notice from the Personnel Department that he will be eligible for retirement within 80 months. How many years before Tom can retire?

a. 8 years

b. 6 years, 8 months

c. 6 1/2 years

d. None of the above

14. Carlos Demonte needs to connect two offices using fiber optic cables. The two offices are 5.6 miles apart. How many feet of cable will be needed to connect these two offices?

a. 9,856 feet

b. 29,568 feet

c. 5,280 feet

d. None of the above

15. Midway Medical Research Center sponsored an employee Walk-a-Thon to raise funding for research. Employees received pledges for each mile they walked. Twelve sponsors each pledged $10.00 per mile. The employees walked a combined total of 55 miles. How much money was raised through the Walk-a-Thon pledges?

a. $6,600.00

b. $660.00

c. $550.00

d. $562.00

16. Rohrmann and Weuner, a law firm, decided to install laser printers in two offices. They will need 31 feet of laser cable for one printer and 47 feet of cable for the other. The printer installer brings 30 yards of cable to install the two printers. Will this be enough to do the job?

   a. Yes

   b. No

17. Wimbledon Book Company is shipping a book order to a school. The shipping charges are based on the weight of the books shipped. Each book weighs 26 ounces. A set of 50 books is being shipped with charges of $.28 per pound. How much are the shipping charges?

   a. $81.25

   b. $22.75

   c. $23.00

   d. $28.00

18. Microtech America is shipping a computer and printer. The computer weighs 48 pounds, 12 ounces, and the printer weighs 24 pounds, 8 ounces. What is the total weight of the shipment?

   a. 72 pounds, 20 ounces

   b. 73 pounds, 8 ounces

   c. 73 pounds, 4 ounces

   d. None of the above

19. Jarvis March is a roofer. He needs enough plywood to cover a roof that is 1,342 square feet. Plywood comes in 4 x 8 foot sheets. How many plywood sheets should Jarvis order for the job?

   a. 47

   b. 42

   c. 1,370

   d. 1,314

20. Eastland Photo Labs shipped two packages. One package weighed 5 pounds, 9 ounces, and the other package weighed 14 pounds, 12 ounces. What was the total weight of the shipment?

   a. 20 pounds, 5 ounces

   b. 21 pounds, 5 ounces

   c. 19 pounds, 9 ounces

   d. None of the above

21. Rhonda's Boutique purchased 9 reams of paper for their laser printer. Total weight of the 9 reams of paper was 18 pounds, 9 ounces. How much did each ream of paper weigh?

   a. 9 pounds, 4 ounces

   b. 2 pounds, 1 ounce

   c. 2 pounds, 9 ounces

   d. 9 pounds

22. River City decided to put Christmas lights along the city streets, a distance of 9.6 miles. One company bid $32,000 for the job. A second company bid $.60 per foot for the job. A third company bid $1 per yard for the job. Which bid is lowest?

   a. First company

   b. Second company

   c. Third company

   d. Lowest bid cannot be determined

23. Global Freight Lines uses trucks to deliver shipments between Arkansas and Memphis. For one shipment, 240 packages weighing 25 pounds each are being loaded. What is the total weight of this shipment?

   a. 6,000 tons

   b. 25 tons

   c. 3 tons

   d. None of the above

24. The McCoy Company shipped 36 word processors. Each word processor weighed 6 pounds, 4 ounces. What was the total weight of the shipment?

    a. 6 pounds, 9 ounces

    b. 225 pounds

    c. 216 pounds

    d. 42 pounds, 4 ounces

25. Lanston Company shipped 12 items. The total weight of the 12 items was 6 pounds, 3 ounces. An item weighing 11 ounces was lost. What was the weight of the remaining items?

    a. 2 pounds, 4 ounces

    b. 6 pounds, 14 ounces

    c. 5 pounds, 14 ounces

    d. 5 pounds, 8 ounces

UNIT IV

EXTRA PRACTICE EXERCISES

Extra Practice Exercises

Workplace problems in this unit will present various math operations that were presented in the first three units of this program. Read and solve the following problems. Remember that only one answer is correct. Where appropriate, reduce values to lowest terms.

1. Multiply: 27.84 x 6.05 percent = ?

   a. 1.68432

   b. 16.8432

   c. 168.432

   d. 1,684.32

2. Divide: $37.20 / 12 = ?

   a. $31

   b. $3.10

   c. $0.31

   d. $0.12

3. Multiply: $224 x 7 1/2 = ?

   a. $168

   b. $1,678

   c. $1,680

   d. $1,692

4. Add: 8 hours, 40 minutes + 12 hours, 50 minutes = ?

   a. 20 hours, 40 minutes

   b. 20 hours, 50 minutes

   c. 21 hours, 30 minutes

   d. 21 hours, 45 minutes

5. What is the ratio: 300 to 20 = ?

    a. 3:2

    b. 30:1

    c. 20:1

    d. 15:1

6. City Security Services provides quotes for stock prices. One stock, AMZ Corp., is quoted at $37.5. A second stock, GHY, Inc., is quoted at $23.625. What is the difference in the price quotes for the two stocks?

    a. $13.875

    b. $61.125

    c. $13.125

    d. $37.50

7. Mike Grimes is a sales clerk at Graphic Art Supplies. During the past five days, his sales were as follows: $123.45, $143.89, $189.50, $139.42, and $120.51. What was the amount of Mike's total sales for the five days?

    a. $596.26

    b. $716.77

    c. $714.00

    d. None of the above

8. Sarah Rodriguez is a payroll clerk for Danker Video Co. What paycheck amount should Sarah compute for an employee with the following data: Regular earnings, $592.54 and overtime earnings, $83.59? Deductions were $44.25 for FICA taxes and $109.25 for federal withholding taxes.

    a. $676.13

    b. $153.50

    c. $522.63

    d. $829.63

9. Kim Hayakawa is an office assistant at Rad Motors. A used car that cost the company $10,218 is sold for $8,935.58. The salesperson is paid $200 commission to sell the car. What is the loss on the sale of the car?

    a. $10,218

    b. $1,282.42

    c. $1,482.42

    d. $1,082.42

10. Abdul Labar works part-time at Zenith Bicycles. He sold 12 bicycles during the week. Each Model Z128 cost $175.24 and sold for $235.84. What was the total profit for the 12 bicycles?

   a. $60.60
   b. $5.05
   c. $727.20
   d. $4,932.96

11. Dominic Fosco is a supervisor at Carter Chair Factory. The employees built 8 chairs per hour yesterday during an 8-hour shift. Today, the same employees built 9 chairs per hour during an 8-hour shift. The company goal was to build 130 chairs in the 2 days. Was Dominic able to report that his crew met the company goal?

   a. Yes
   b. No

12. Cyril Chang is an accounting clerk at Creative Games Company. A department head says, "I need to purchase 11 SX486 computers for $1,989 each. Do we have enough money in our budget to buy them?" Cyril checked the budget and found that the department has $21,000. Is this enough?

   a. Yes
   b. No

13. Graphic Designs decided to convert their records to an electronic database system. A local company agreed to enter the records for $.085 each. There were 900 records entered on Monday and 400 records entered on Tuesday. What was the data entry cost for the job?

   a. $1,300.085
   b. $110.50
   c. $1,105
   d. $11.05

14. Don Ponce is a salesperson at the Active Sports Spa. Don's job is to sell memberships at $425 each. Last week, he sold 52 memberships. Under his contract, he has the option of receiving a $300 weekly salary or a commission equal to 1.5 percent of the dollar amount of the memberships sold. Which option will give the most pay?

   a. Weekly salary
   b. Commission

15. Larry Loos works in the order department at National Office Supply. An order was received from Bortex Manufacturing for 24 legal pads costing $.50 each and 18 disk storage boxes costing $14.95 each. What amount should Larry bill Bortex?

   a. $12
   b. $269.10
   c. $281.10
   d. $257.10

16. The accounting department ordered 144 computer disks. The finance department ordered 48 computer disks. A sales catalog lists disks at $18.60 per box with 12 disks in each box. What was the cost of the order?

   a. $297.60
   b. $223.20
   c. $74.40
   d. $3,571.20

17. Next month, Easy Tax Company's West Street office will need 185 computer disks. The Olive Street office will need 211 disks. There are 32 dozen disks in stock. Is this enough disks?

   a. Yes
   b. No

18. Kiner's law firm wants to send gift briefcases to 1,200 clients. Crouch Company's bid was $24.95 per briefcase. Smith Office Supply agreed to supply 1,200 briefcases for $30,000. The Import House will supply the first 500 briefcases for $32.85 each and the remaining 700 briefcases for $27.50 each. Which company has the lowest price?

   a. Smith Office Supply
   b. Crouch Company
   c. Import House

19. Bertha Thompson is a clerk typist for Paul's Department Store. Her regular earnings last year were $20,000. She earned an additional $4,000 working overtime. Bertha saved $2,000 during the year. Her rent expenses were $5,000. What portion of Bertha's total income was represented by savings?

   a. 1/2
   b. 1/4
   c. 1/10
   d. 1/12

20. Donna McComas is a clerk in the admissions office at Bailey Business School. Last year, 400 of 600 applicants for the freshman class were accepted. Also, 300 of 400 applicants for the sophomore class were accepted. The director says, "Donna, what fraction of the total number of freshman and sophomore applicants were accepted at Bailey Business School?"

    a. 7/10
    b. 2/3
    c. 3/4
    d. None of the above

21. Mr. Benz, Ms. Mauz, and Mr. Ruiz formed a partnership. Last year, their company made a $144,000 profit. Mr. Benz is to receive $46,000 or 1/3 of the profit, whichever is larger. Which option is best for Mr. Benz this year?

    a. $46,000
    b. 1/3 of the profit

22. Alicia Bonito, a welder, has the option of earning $225 per week or $8.60 per hour, whichever is larger. She worked 7 1/2 hours on Monday, 6 1/4 hours on Tuesday, 7 3/4 hours on Thursday, and 6 3/4 hours on Friday. Which plan will be best for Alicia?

    a. $225 per week
    b. $8.60 per hour

23. Ginger Crowley is a purchasing agent at Tower Type-All. A company agreed to sell Tower 4 word processors at a 30 percent discount. The original price, before the discount, was $270 each. Ginger computed the discount. What was the total discount for the word processors?

    a. $1,080
    b. $81
    c. $324
    d. $900

24. Grogan Construction Company's total operating expenses for the past week were $4,800. A $1,200 equipment rental expense was included in this amount. What percent of the total operating expenses was equipment rental?

    a. 250 percent
    b. 25 percent
    c. 400 percent
    d. $1,200

25. Paul Hobart is a computer programmer with National Air Express. His annual salary is $38,500. Paul was offered a 12.5 percent increase to stay with National. A competing company offered him a $42,000 annual salary. What decision should Paul make to earn the highest annual salary?

   a. Stay with National

   b. Move to the competing company

26. Carlos Perez is a quality control specialist with Townsend Manufacturing. In his sampling of 300 completed products, 6 were found to be defective. According to the industry standard, a 1 percent or less defective rate is acceptable. Is Townsend meeting acceptable standards?

   a. Yes

   b. No

27. Doone Electronics produces a chip needed by remote control televisions. The company employs 20 technicians who produce a total of 800 chips each day. The company wants to increase production to 1,000 chips per day. How many technicians will be needed to meet this increased production schedule?

   a. 25

   b. 40

   c. 40,000

   d. 50

28. Brad Caustis works as a mortgage analyst for Dawn Financial Services. A client making a $3,000 monthly salary wants to know if she can qualify for an $84,000 mortgage for a new house. The mortgage can be up to two and one-half times annual income. Does the client qualify for the mortgage?

   a. Yes

   b. No

29. Rex Martin is a salesperson for Victory Video. His sales last month were $42,000. Rex was awarded a $735 bonus based on the percent of sales during the month. What was the bonus percent for his monthly sales?

   a. 17.5 percent

   b. 1.75 percent

   c. 0.175 percent

   d. 0.0175 percent

30. Vu Chang is an administrative secretary for Mama's Pizza. Her salary is $12.50 per hour. Last week she worked 7 3/4 hours on Monday, 7 1/2 hours on Tuesday, 8 hours on Wednesday, 7 1/4 hours on Thursday, and 8 hours on Friday. What were Vu's earnings for the week?

    a. $38.50
    b. $12.50
    c. $481.25
    d. $4,812.50

31. Lynn McCormick is shopping for a new car. EZ Auto Sales offered a sports car to Lynn under the following terms: $350 payment per month for 3 1/2 years. Best Deal Auto Sales offered a similar car to Lynn under the following terms: $80 per week for 3 1/2 years. Which offer gives Lynn the lowest total cost?

    a. EZ Auto Sales
    b. Best Deal Auto Sales

32. Carla Hoffman works for a company that installs cable for computer networks. She is asked to install 37 feet of cable in one room and 59 feet of cable in a second room. She has 30 yards of cable. Will this be enough to do the job?

    a. Yes
    b. No

33. Holiday Country Club decided to install a new fence around the golf course, a distance of 1.5 miles. Design Fence Company agreed to do the job for $3.50 per foot. Safenet Fence Company agreed to do the job for $10 per yard. AAA Fence Company agreed to do the job for $27,000. Which company offered the lowest price?

    a. Design Fence Company
    b. Safenet Fence Company
    c. AAA Fence Company

34. Hasty Print printed 200 copies of a catalog for a company located in Los Angeles. Each catalog weighed 2 pounds, 4 ounces. Champion Freight Services agreed to ship the items for $.75 per pound. Express Now agreed to ship the entire order for $350. Which carrier offered the lowest price?

    a. Champion Freight Services
    b. Express Now

35. Grange Freight Lines uses a small truck to deliver packages for a $100 per load charge. City Office Supply requested that 300 packages, weighing 35 pounds each, be delivered. The capacity of the delivery truck is 3 tons. How much will City Office Supply be charged for the entire shipment?

   a. $100

   b. $200

   c. $300

   d. $400

Answers and Explanations, see page 200.

PART TWO

ANSWERS
AND
EXPLANATIONS

SECTION 1: Addition and Subtraction

Quick Check

1. b	10. b	19. a
2. d	11. b	20. b
3. c	12. c	21. d
4. a	13. b	22. a
5. c	14. c	23. b
6. b	15. d	24. a
7. b	16. c	25. b
8. d	17. d	
9. a	18. b	

Explanations

1. b

2. d

3. c

4. a

5. c

6. a. Incorrect. You found the number of pages in the report equals 50.

   b. Correct.

   c. Incorrect. You found only the number of copies needed by the first department, 5.

   d. Incorrect. You found only the number of copies needed by the second department, 3.

   Explanation: The total number of copies needed is found by adding the copies needed by each department (5 + 3 + 7 = 15).

7. a. Incorrect. You found only the number of freshman students, 645.

   b. Correct.

   c. Incorrect. You found only the number of male students, 1,338.

   d. Incorrect. You calculated the number of male and female students, 2,660.

   Explanation: The number of female students is found by adding the enrollment figures for the female column (325 + 389 + 319 + 289 = 1,322). The total number of female students equals 1,322.

8.   a. Incorrect. You found the number of freshman students, 645.

    b. Incorrect. You found the number of female students, 1,322.

    c. Incorrect. You found the number of male students, 1,338.

    d. Correct.

    Explanation: The total number of students is found by adding all values in the table. The total number of students equals 2,660.

9.   a. Correct.

    b. Incorrect. She exceeded the $400 goal.

    Explanation: Yesterday's sales are found by adding the sales amounts ($123.45 + $67.43 + $29.29 + $109.42 + $72.48 = $402.07).

10. a. Inorrect.

    b. Correct.

    Explanation: The number of ribbons is found by adding the amount of each product number in inventory (145 + 107 + 157 = 409).

11. a. Incorrect. You must have added the scores incorrectly.

    b. Correct.

    c. Incorrect. You omitted the values to the right of the decimal place.

    d. Incorrect. You must have added the scores incorrectly.

    Explanation: The total is found by adding the three scores (28.05 + 36.4 + 30.003 = 94.453).

12. a. Incorrect. The hours were added incorrectly.

    b. Incorrect. The hours must have been added incorrectly.

    c. Correct.

    d. Incorrect. The hours must have been added incorrectly.

    Explanation: Total hours is found by adding the hours worked each day (6.5 + 7.25 + 8.5 + 7.75 + 8 = 38).

13. a. Incorrect. The total amount is greater than the desired $2,000 price.

    b. Correct.

    Explanation: Total supplies is found by adding the individual amounts ($1,899.75 + $79.28 + $27.55 = $2,006.58).

14. a. Incorrect. You added the deductions to the total earnings instead of subtracting.

    b. Incorrect. You did not subtract the deductions.

    c. Correct.

    d. Incorrect.

Explanation: Total earnings is found by adding the earnings amounts ($872.45 + $75.89 = $948.34). The deduction is then subtracted from total earnings to determine net pay ($948.34 − $147.25 = $801.09).

15. a. Incorrect. The number of hours open has no relation to available number of employees.
    b. Incorrect. The time open each day has no relation to available number of employees.
    c. Incorrect. The number of branch offices has no relation to available number of employees.
    d. Correct.

Explanation: If you know the total number of employees, you can subtract the number that were out sick (3) from the total to find the number of employees who were at work.

16. a. Incorrect. You added the number that were sold to the number remaining.
    b. Incorrect. You did not subtract the number sold during the time period from the number available.
    c. Correct.
    d. Incorrect. The number sold during the period equals 4, not the number remaining.

Explanation: The number remaining is found by subtracting the number sold from the number available (23 − 4 = 19).

17. a. Incorrect. You added the number of years worked to the number of years needed for retirement.
    b. Incorrect. You did not subtract the number of years worked.
    c. Incorrect. You chose the number of years worked without subtracting it from the number of years needed for retirement.
    d. Correct.

Explanation: Find the years remaining by subtracting the years worked from the number of years needed for retirement (30 − 19 = 11).

18. a. Incorrect. You added instead of subtracting the number of gloves produced so far this month.
    b. Correct.
    c. Incorrect. The normal production is 738 gloves. You did not subtract the number produced so far.
    d. Incorrect. The company is normally open 6 days per week, which has no relation to the requested answer.

Explanation: The number of gloves remaining for the month is found by subtracting the number produced from the number normally produced (738 − 149 = 589).

19. a. Correct.

b. Incorrect. You found the total earnings but did not subtract the total deductions.

c. Incorrect. You found only the total deductions.

d. Incorrect. You added the total deductions.

Explanation: Total earnings is found by adding the earnings amounts ($589.24 + $72.45 = $661.69). Total deductions is found by adding the deductions amounts ($41.50 + $104.35 = $145.85). Net pay is found by subtracting total deductions from total earnings ($661.69 − $145.85 = $515.84).

20. a. Incorrect. You did not subtract the total returns from the total sales.

b. Correct.

c. Incorrect. Your choice represents the total returns, which should be subtracted from the total sales.

d. Incorrect. You added the total sales and returns instead of subtracting.

Explanation: Total sales is found by adding the sales amounts ($135.34 + $275.34 + $309.28 + $198.30 = $918.26). Total returns is found by adding the return amounts ($37.85 + $27.61 = $65.46). Net sales is found by subtracting total returns from total sales ($918.26 − $65.46 = $852.80).

21. a. Incorrect. You added the total sales and returns instead of subtracting.

b. Incorrect. You incorrectly rounded the answer to a whole number after subtracting the purchase price from the sales price.

c. Incorrect. You should not have rounded the answer to one place to the right of the decimal after subtracting the purchase price from the sales price.

d. Correct.

Explanation: The purchase price should be subtracted from the sales price to find the increase ($52.5 − $37.875 = $14.625).

22. a. Correct.

b. Incorrect.

Explanation: The sales price minus the cost price gives you the profit for each item as follows: (TV: $975.85 − $635.84 = $340.01) (VCR: $307.50 − $189.75 = $117.75). Total profit is then found by adding the profit amounts for the two items ($340.01 + $117.75 = $457.76). This total profit on the TV and VCR exceeds the $450 profit goal.

23. a. Incorrect.

    b. Correct.

    c. Incorrect. You did not subtract the withdrawal.

    d. Incorrect. All the necessary information is available.

Explanation: Deposits are added to the beginning balance to find the amount available ($875.92 + $275.89 + $304.55 = $1,456.36). The withdrawal should be subtracted from the amount available to find the ending balance ($1,456.36 − $325.45 = $1,130.91).

24. a. Correct.

    b. Incorrect. You found only the cost of the car to the company.

    c. Incorrect. You forgot to include the sales commission as part of the cost of the car.

    d. Incorrect.

Explanation: Find the cost to the company by adding the purchase price of the car plus commission ($8,756.25 + $123.89 = $8,880.14). Then subtract this amount from the sales price to determine the profit ($12,389.25 − $8,880.14 = $3,509.11).

25. a. Incorrect.

    b. Correct.

Explanation: The new line provides only a $23.13 profit ($312.58 minus $289.45) while the old line provides a $32.40 profit ($307.25 minus $274.85).

SECTION 2: Multiplication

1. b	10. c	19. b
2. d	11. c	20. c
3. c	12. a	21. a
4. a	13. d	22. a
5. c	14. c	23. b
6. c	15. d	24. b
7. b	16. a	25. b
8. c	17. b	
9. a	18. c	

Explanations

1. b
2. d
3. c
4. a
5. c
6. a. Incorrect.
   b. Incorrect.
   c. Correct.
   d. Incorrect.

   Explanation: Multiply the number of hours by the hourly rate to find the total earnings (38 x $15 = $570).

7. a. Incorrect.
   b. Correct.

   Explanation: Multiply the envelopes that can be addressed per hour times the number of hours to find the number of envelopes that can be addressed during the 8-hour period (180 x 8 = 1,440). Barbara would not be able to address the 1,500 envelopes in 8 hours.

8. a. Incorrect. You multiplied the number of office chairs manufactured per minute by the number of hours.
   b. Incorrect. You failed to multiply the chairs manufactured in 1 hour by the number of hours.

c. Correct.

d. Incorrect.

Explanation: The number of office chairs manufactured in 1 minute is multiplied by 60 to find the number of chairs manufactured in 1 hour (2 x 60 = 120). This amount is then multiplied by 3 to find the number of chairs manufactured in 3 hours (120 x 3 = 360).

9. a. Correct.

b. Incorrect.

Explanation: The cost of the purchase is found by multiplying the cost per computer by the number of computers to be purchased (9 x $1,584 = $14,256). Since this amount is less than the $15,000 budgeted amount, the equipment can be purchased.

10. a. Incorrect. This response gives the earnings for only 1 week—40 hours.

b. Incorrect. By adding the earnings per hour to the number of hours per week, you have calculated an incorrect hourly pay rate.

c. Correct.

d. Incorrect. By adding the earnings per hour to the hours per week, you have calculated an incorrect hourly pay rate.

Explanation: Find the number of hours worked by multiplying the number of weeks by the number of hours worked per week. Then multiply the number of hours worked by the rate earned per hour.

11. a. Incorrect. You multiplied the number of boxes shipped during a year by the cost to ship each box.

b. Incorrect. You performed the correct computation but placed the decimal point one too many places to the right in the answer.

c. Correct.

d. Incorrect.

Explanation: The number of boxes shipped should be multiplied by the cost to ship each box (230 x $2.875 = $661.25).

12. a. Correct.

b. Incorrect.

Explanation: Multiply the number of records produced each day by the work days per week to find the number of records produced each week (1,800 x 5 = 9,000). Then, multiply by the cost per record to find the proposed data entry cost (9,000 x $.075 = $675). Since this amount is higher than the $600 current cost, it will cost more to hire a local company.

13. a. Incorrect. You multiplied 10 times 35—without regard to decimal places.

 b. Incorrect. You divided the number of sheets printed by 10.

 c. Incorrect. You completed the correct computation but placed the decimal point one place too far to the right in the answer.

 d. Correct.

 Explanation: The laser cost is found by multiplying the cost per sheet by the number of sheets ($.035 x 5,000 = $175).

14. a. Incorrect. You completed the correct computation but placed the decimal point one place too far to the left in the answer and then rounded down.

 b. Incorrect. You completed the correct computation but placed the decimal point one place too far to the left in the answer and then rounded up.

 c. Correct.

 d. Incorrect. You completed the correct computation but placed the decimal point one place too far to the right.

 Explanation: The amount due is found by multiplying the number of units by the rate per unit (1,758 x $.175 = $307.65).

15. a. Incorrect. You did not include the price of the computer disk boxes in your computation.

 b. Incorrect. You did not include the price of the legal pads in your computation.

 c. Incorrect. You subtracted the price of the legal pads from the price of the computer disk boxes.

 d. Correct.

 Explanation: The total amount is found by multiplying the quantity of each item by the price (30 x $.50 = $15.00; 12 x $14.95 = $179.40). Then, add the price of the legal pads to the price of the computer disk boxes ($15.00 + $179.40 = $194.40).

16. a. Correct.

 b. Incorrect. You completed the correct computation but placed the decimal point one place too far to the left in your answer.

 c. Incorrect. You multiplied the number of rolls sold each month by the cost per roll.

 d. Incorrect.

 Explanation: The value of the tape in inventory is found by multiplying the number of rolls in inventory by the cost per roll (11,245 x $.50 = $5622.50).

17. a. Incorrect. You added the cost of 1 chair to the normal annual purchases.

    b. Correct.

    c. Incorrect. You included the price of only 1 chair.

    d. Incorrect. You subtracted the cost of the order from the normal annual purchases.

Explanation: The cost of the order is found by multiplying the number of chairs purchased by the cost per chair (3 x $339.95 = $1,019.85).

18. a. Incorrect. You subtracted the amount used from the annual purchase amount.

    b. Incorrect. You added the amount used to the annual purchase amount.

    c. Correct.

    d. Incorrect. You subtracted the amount used so far from the additional money needed.

Explanation: The additional money needed is found by multiplying the number of additional cases by the cost per case (225 x $25.50 = $5,737.50).

19. a. Incorrect.

    b. Correct.

Explanation: The number of pencils is multiplied by the price per pencil to find the price provided by Best Co. (7,500 x $.50 = $3,750). This price is lower than the $4,000 price provided by Ace Co.

20. a. Incorrect. You multiplied the hourly salary rate by 40.

    b. Incorrect. You multiplied the normal hours per week by 37.5.

    c. Correct.

    d. Incorrect.

Explanation: The earnings are found by multiplying the number of hours Harold worked by the hourly salary rate (37.5 x $7.70 = $288.75).

21. a. Correct.

    b. Incorrect.

Explanation: The cost of the forms on a per unit basis is found by multiplying the number of forms by the cost per form (180,000 x $.015 = $2,700). Since this amount is less than the $2,750 total price proposed, the proposal on a cost per form basis is the lowest one.

22. a. Correct.

    b. Incorrect.

    Explanation: The cost for the space on a per square foot basis from the company in Los Angeles is found by multiplying the total space by the cost per square foot (15,782 x $.655 = $10,337.21). Since this amount is less than the $12,000 proposal from the company in San Francisco, the proposal from Los Angeles is the lowest.

23. a. Incorrect. You multiplied the records entered by experienced personnel by the rate per record.

    b. Correct.

    c. Incorrect. You completed the correct computation but placed the decimal point one place too far to the right in the answer.

    d. Incorrect. You multiplied the records entered by experienced personnel by the rate per record and then placed the decimal point one place too far to the right in the answer.

    Explanation: The earnings are computed by multiplying the number of records entered by the rate per record (824 x $.075 = $61.80).

24. a. Incorrect. You computed only the cost using the daisy wheel printer.

    b. Correct.

    c. Incorrect. You computed only the cost using the laser printer.

    d. Incorrect.

    Explanation: The daisy printer costs are found by multiplying the number of copies by the cost per copy (5,000 x $.10 = $500). The laser printer costs are found by multiplying the number of copies by the cost per copy (5,000 x $.04 = $200). The difference represents the savings between the two methods ($500 – $200 = $300).

25. a. Incorrect.

    b. Correct.

    Explanation: The commission is found by multiplying the sales by the commission rate ($92,500 x .015 = $1,387.50). This amount is higher than the $975 weekly salary.

SECTION 3: Division

1. b	10. d	19. c
2. d	11. d	20. b
3. c	12. b	21. d
4. a	13. a	22. c
5. b	14. c	23. a
6. b	15. b	24. d
7. c	16. b	25. d
8. c	17. b	
9. b	18. a	

Explanations

1. b
2. d
3. c
4. a
5. b
6. a. Incorrect.
   b. Correct.

   Explanation: The amount remaining, divided by the cost per ribbon, gives you the number of ribbons that can be purchased with remaining funds ($1,875 / 15 = 125). Therefore, enough funds remain to purchase only 125 additional ribbons.

7. a. Incorrect. You multiplied instead of dividing.
   b. Incorrect. You added instead of dividing.
   c. Correct.
   d. Incorrect. You subtracted instead of dividing.

   Explanation: Divide the number of sales by the number of hours to compute the number of sales per hour (222 / 6 = 37).

8. a. Incorrect. You multiplied instead of dividing.
   b. Incorrect. You added instead of dividing.
   c. Correct.
   d. Incorrect. You subtracted instead of dividing.

Explanation: The number of pallets needed is found by dividing the total cartons by the number of cartons that fit on a pallet (1152 / 64 = 18).

9. a. Incorrect. You divided the total number of customers by the number of accountants instead of the number of marketing representatives.

   b. Correct.

   c. Incorrect. You divided the number of marketing representatives by the number of accountants.

   d. Incorrect. You added instead of dividing.

Explanation: The number of customers to assign to each representative is found by dividing the total number of customers by the number of representatives (6,720 / 240 = 28).

10. a. Incorrect. You added the number of participants to the number of seminars.

   b. Incorrect. You subtracted the number of seminars from the number of participants.

   c. Incorrect. You divided the number of participants by the number of different businesses.

   d. Correct.

Explanation: The average number of participants attending each seminar is found by dividing the total number of participants by the number of seminars offered (960 / 32 = 30).

11. a. Incorrect. You divided the cost per box by the number of computers.

   b. Incorrect. You multiplied the cost per box by the number of disks per box.

   c. Incorrect. You added the cost per box to the number of disks in a box.

   d. Correct.

Explanation: The cost per disk is found by dividing the cost per box by the number of disks in the box ($18.72 / 12 = $1.56).

12. a. Incorrect. This value is lower than the 16 miles per gallon average for the fleet.

   b. Correct.

Explanation: The miles per gallon, 15.8, is found by dividing the number of miles driven by the number of gallons of gasoline used (120,080 / 7,600 = 15.8). This value is lower than the 16 miles per gallon fleet average.

13. a. Correct.

   b. Incorrect.

   c. Incorrect.

   d. Incorrect.

Explanation: To check the computation, multiply the answer found by the number being divided by to determine if this answer equals the number being divided into in the division problem (8 x 377 = 3,016).

14. a. Incorrect. You found only the total expenses, not the average.

    b. Incorrect. You multiplied the total expenses by the number of employees instead of dividing.

    c. Correct.

    d. Incorrect.

    Explanation: The average cost per employee is found by adding the expenses and then dividing the total by the number of employees ($790.16 / 4 = $197.54).

15. a. Incorrect. You divided the weekly salary by the number of employees.

    b. Correct.

    c. Incorrect. You multiplied the weekly salary by the number of hours worked.

    d. Incorrect. You added the weekly salary and the number of employees.

    Explanation: The amount earned per hour is found by dividing the weekly salary by the number of hours worked ($462 / 52.5 = $8.80).

16. a. Incorrect. You completed the correct computation, but placed the decimal point one place too far to the right in your answer.

    b. Correct.

    c. Incorrect. You completed the correct computation, but placed the decimal point one place too far to the left in your answer.

    d. Incorrect.

    Explanation: The bonus per employee is found by dividing the total bonus money by the number of representatives ($55,646 / 24 = $2,318.58).

17. a. Incorrect. The average is 59.34. Two of the scores were above this value—62.5 and 60.4.

    b. Correct.

    c. Incorrect. The average is 59.34. Two of the scores were above this value—62.5 and 60.4.

    d. Incorrect.

    Explanation: The average score is found by dividing the total of the scores by the number of scores (296.7 / 5 = 59.34).

18. a. Correct.

b. Incorrect. You divided the number of file folders used each week by the number of file folders per box.

c. Incorrect. You divided the number of file folders used each week by the number of boxes of file folders.

d. Incorrect. You multiplied the total number of file folders by the number used each week.

Explanation: First find the total number of file folders by multiplying the number of boxes by the number of file folders per box (12 x 25 = 300). The total number of file folders is then divided by the number used each week to compute the number of weeks the file folders will last (300 / 40 = 7.5).

19. a. Incorrect. You completed the correct computation but placed the decimal point two places too far to the right in your answer.

b. Incorrect. You completed the correct computation but placed the decimal point one place too far to the right in your answer.

c. Correct.

d. Incorrect. You completed the correct computation, but placed the decimal point one place too far to the left in your answer.

Explanation: The labor cost per unit is found by dividing the salary by the number of units produced ($425.20 / 25,500 = .0167).

20. a. Incorrect. You would have ordered only 192 with this response (12 x 16 = 192).

b. Correct.

c. Incorrect. You would have ordered only 144 with this response (12 x 12 = 144).

d. Incorrect. You would have ordered too many with this response (12 x 20 = 240).

Explanation: The number of dozen needed is found by dividing the number ordered by 12 (200 / 12 = 16.66, rounded to 16.7). Since orders are by the dozen, the next highest number must be ordered—17.

21. a. Incorrect. You divided the weekly earnings by the number of working days in a week.

b. Incorrect. You divided the weekly earnings by the percent deduction.

c. Incorrect. You divided the accumulation goal by the deduction percent.

d. Correct.

Explanation: Find the number of weeks needed to meet her goal by dividing the goal by the amount contributed each week ($3,000 / 48 = 62.5). Since she is paid by the week, the deduction for 63 weeks will be needed to reach her $3,000 goal.

22. a. Incorrect. You completed the correct computation but placed the decimal point one place too far to the left in your answer.
    b. Incorrect. You multiplied instead of dividing.
    c. Correct.
    d. Incorrect.

    Explanation: The number of weeks is found by dividing the total contribution by the contribution per week ($98 / $.80 = 122.5).

23. a. Correct.
    b. Incorrect.

    Explanation: Find the cost per page by dividing the weekly salary by the number of pages that can be formatted ($315 / 150 = $2.10). This amount is less than the $2.25 per page goal.

24. a. Incorrect.
    b. Incorrect.
    c. Incorrect.
    d. Correct.

    Explanation: Find the average age by dividing the total ages by the number of computers (23.4 / 5 = 4.68).

25. a. Incorrect. You divided the total price by the number of ribbons in a dozen.
    b. Incorrect. You divided the total price by the number of boxes purchased.
    c. Incorrect. You divided the total price by the number of boxes purchased and placed the decimal point one place too far to the left.
    d. Correct.

    Explanation: First, find the total number of ribbons purchased by multiplying the number of boxes by the number of ribbons per box (24 x 12 = 288). The price per ribbon is computed by dividing the total price by the number of ribbons purchased ($1,800 / 288 = $6.25).

SECTION 4: Combination Problems

1. b	10. b	19. b
2. c	11. d	20. a
3. b	12. b	21. b
4. d	13. d	22. c
5. c	14. a	23. a
6. a	15. a	24. a
7. d	16. c	25. a
8. d	17. b	
9. c	18. c	

Explanations

1. b
2. c
3. b
4. d
5. c
6. a. Correct.
   b. Incorrect. You included only the staplers sold during January.
   c. Incorrect. You included only the staplers sold during February.
   d. Incorrect. You included only the staplers sold during the first week.

   Explanation: All values should be added to find the total.

7. a. Incorrect. You added the total deductions to the total earnings.
   b. Incorrect. You found only total earnings, without subtracting total deductions.
   c. Incorrect. You found only total deductions, without subtracting these deductions from the total earnings.
   d. Correct.

   Explanation: The total deductions should be subtracted from the total earnings to find the net pay ($596.24 − $149.48 = $446.76).

8. a. Incorrect. You completed the correct computation, but placed the decimal point one place too far to the left in the answer.
   b. Incorrect. You found only the cost per box.

c. Incorrect. You found the cost per box correctly in the first step, but divided by 14 instead of multiplying by 14 in the last step.

d. Correct.

Explanation: The cost per box is found by multiplying the cost per disk by the number of disks in a box ($2.16 x 10 = $21.60). The cost of the order is found by multiplying the cost per box by the number of boxes ordered ($21.60 x 14 = $302.40).

9. a. Incorrect. You multiplied the cost per box by the number of weeks.

b. Incorrect. You multiplied the number of boxes used every 2 weeks by the number of weeks and then multiplied this answer by the cost per box.

c. Correct.

d. Incorrect.

Explanation: The number of boxes used per week is found by dividing the number of boxes used in 2 weeks by the number of weeks (3 / 2 = 1.5). Then the number of boxes needed during a 24-week period is found by multiplying the number used per week by 24 (1.5 x 24 = 36). Finally, the total cost is found by multiplying the cost per box by the number of boxes used ($2.23 x 36 = $80.28).

10. a. Incorrect. You completed the correct computation but placed the decimal point one place too far to the right.

b. Correct.

c. Incorrect. You multiplied the number of weeks by 100.

d. Incorrect. You divided the number of folders by the cost per folder.

Explanation: The total price is found by multiplying the number of folders by the cost per folder (1,200 x $.075 = $90).

11. a. Incorrect. You forgot to include the $40 delivery fee.

b. Incorrect. You included only the cost of the executive chairs.

c. Incorrect. You subtracted the $40 delivery fee instead of adding.

d. Correct.

Explanation: First, multiply the cost of each item by the number of items (chairs: $339.95 x 2 = $679.90; cabinets: $99.95 x 3 = $299.85). Delivery charges ($40) are then added to these two amounts to find total cost of the order ($679.90 + $299.85 + $40 = $1,019.75).

12. a. Incorrect. Meryl made $388.83. This amount is less than the $390 goal.

b. Correct.

Explanation: Total pay is found by multiplying the hours worked by the pay rate per hour (39 x $9.97 = $388.83).

13. a. Incorrect.

    b. Incorrect.

    c. Incorrect.

    d. Correct.

Explanation: The price of the order is found by multiplying the number of items by the unit price.

14. a. Correct.

    b. Incorrect. You multiplied the total pay by the number of employees.

    c. Incorrect. You divided the total pay by the number of years of operation.

    d. Incorrect. You divided the correct answer by the number of years of operation.

Explanation: The average pay is found by dividing the total pay by the number of employees ($2,741.22 / 9 = $304.58).

15. a. Correct.

    b. Incorrect.

Explanation: The estimate is found by rounding the number of clients to 2,800 and dividing by 4 (2,800 / 4 = 700).

16. a. Incorrect. You divided the total amount available by the cost for a full dozen, 12 pencils.

    b. Incorrect. You completed the correct computation but placed the decimal point one place too far to the left in the answer.

    c. Correct.

    d. Incorrect.

Explanation: Find the cost per pencil by dividing the cost for a dozen by 12 ($.96 / 12 = $.08). The number that can be ordered is then found by dividing the total amount available by the cost per pencil (48 / .08 = 600).

17. a. Incorrect. You completed the correct computation but placed the decimal point one place too far to the right in the answer.

    b. Correct.

    c. Incorrect. You completed the correct computation but placed the decimal point one place too far to the left in the answer.

    d. Incorrect. You divided the total units produced by the price per unit.

Explanation: The day's pay is found by multiplying the number of disks packaged by the pay per unit (9,600 x $.0085 = $81.60).

18. a. Incorrect. You found only the number of digits input in an hour.
   b. Incorrect. You completed the first step correctly but divided the number of digits produced in an hour by 8.
   c. Correct.
   d. Incorrect. You multiplied the number of digits input per minute by 8.

   Explanation: Find the total digits input in an hour by multiplying the total digits input in a minute by 60 (212 x 60 = 12,720). Then find the number of digits input in an 8-hour day by multiplying the number of digits input in an hour by 8 (12,720 x 8 = 101,760).

19. a. Incorrect. You completed the correct computation but placed the decimal point one place too far to the right.
   b. Correct.
   c. Incorrect. You completed the correct computation step but placed the decimal point one place too far to the left.
   d. Incorrect. You completed the correct computation but placed the decimal point two places too far to the left.

   Explanation: The bonus is found by multiplying the total salaries by the bonus rate ($820,824.80 x 0.025 = $20,520.62).

20. a. Correct.
   b. Incorrect. The total amount needed is $98,113.92. This amount is less than the $100,000 budgeted amount.

   Explanation: Find total salaries for the 4 additional employees by multiplying the average salary by 4 ($24,528.48 x 4 = $98,113.92).

21. a. Incorrect. You selected only the number of departments as your answer.
   b. Correct.
   c. Incorrect. You found the total cost but did not divide by 3 to determine the cost per department.
   d. Incorrect.

   Explanation: Find the total cost by adding the cost for each department ($875.50 + $1,045.78 + $843.55 = $2,764.83). The total is then divided by 3 to find the amount to be paid by each department ($2,764.83 / 3 = $921.61).

22. a. Incorrect. You completed only the first step needed to solve the problem.
   b. Incorrect. You multiplied the monthly payment by the number of years.
   c. Correct.
   d. Incorrect.

Explanation: Find the total annual payment by multiplying the monthly payment by 12 ($725 x 12 = $8,700). Then find the total payment for the 30-year period by multiplying the annual payment by the number of years ($8,700 x 30 = $261,000).

23. a. Correct.
    b. Incorrect. You found the travel cost for only one way—875 miles.
    c. Incorrect. You computed the first step correctly but divided instead of multiplying in the next step.
    d. Incorrect.

Explanation: Find the total miles by adding the miles each way (875 + 875 = 1,750). Then multiply total miles by the cost per mile (1,750 x $.235 = $411.25).

24. a. Correct.
    b. Incorrect. You forgot to add the commission.
    c. Incorrect. You subtracted the commission from base pay.
    d. Incorrect.

Explanation: Find the base pay by multiplying the number of hours worked by the hourly pay rate (40 x $8.50 = $340). Then add the commission to the base pay ($340 + $75 = $415).

25. a. Correct.
    b. Incorrect. You multiplied the cost per box by the amount on hand.
    c. Incorrect. You multiplied the cost per box by the desired inventory level.
    d. Incorrect. You added the number on hand to the desired total instead of subtracting to determine the number needed to order in the first step.

Explanation: Find the number needed by subtracting the number on hand from the desired total (30 – 7 = 23). Then find the order amount by multiplying the cost per box by the number of items ordered ($14.95 x 23 = $343.85).

SECTION 5: Fractions

1. d	10. a	19. a
2. c	11. d	20. a
3. b	12. b	21. c
4. c	13. b	22. c
5. d	14. d	23. a
6. d	15. c	24. c
7. b	16. a	25. a
8. b	17. a	
9. b	18. a	

Explanations

1. d
2. c
3. b
4. c
5. d
6. a. Incorrect. You reversed the values in the fraction.

   b. Incorrect. You used the sales last year as the part and the expected sales next year as the whole.

   c. Incorrect. You used sales last year as the part and a combination of total sales and foreign sales as the whole.

   d. Correct.

   Explanation: The foreign sales ($2 million) represent the part, and the sales last year ($6 million) represent the whole, which provides the fraction 2/6 (reduced to 1/3).

7. a. Incorrect. You used the number absent last week as the part and the number absent the week before as the whole.

   b. Correct.

   c. Incorrect. You used the number absent last week as the part and the number absent the week before as the whole, with the fraction reduced.

   d. Incorrect. You used the correct procedure, but failed to reduce the fraction to lowest terms.

   Explanation: The number absent last week is the part and total employees represent the whole, which provides the fraction 6/45 (reduced to 2/15).

8. a. Incorrect.

   b. Correct.

   c. Incorrect.

   d. Incorrect.

   Explanation: To reduce a fraction to lowest terms, find a value that can be divided into both the numerator (part) and the denominator (whole) of the fraction.

9. a. Incorrect. You used the government amount as the part of the fraction.

   b. Correct.

   c. Incorrect. You used private donations as the part and the government amount as the whole.

   d. Incorrect.

   Explanation: The private donations represent the part and total donations represent the whole, which provides the fraction 14,000/40,000 (reduced to 7/20).

10. a. Correct.

    b. Incorrect. You used regular pay as the part.

    c. Incorrect. You used overtime pay as the part and regular pay as the whole.

    d. Incorrect.

    Explanation: Total pay is found by adding the regular pay and overtime pay ($18,000 + $6,000 = $24,000). Overtime pay represents the part and total pay represents the whole, which provides the fraction 6,000/24,000 (reduced to 1/4).

11. a. Incorrect. You used the number of roses in yesterday's shipment as the part and the number of roses delivered to date as the whole.

    b. Incorrect. You used the number of roses in yesterday's shipment as the part and the number of roses delivered to date as the whole, without also reducing the fraction to lowest terms.

    c. Incorrect. You followed the correct procedure, but did not reduce the fraction to lowest terms.

    d. Correct.

    Explanation: The number of roses delivered represents the part and total roses ordered represents the whole, which provides the fraction 380/1,900 (reduced to 1/5).

12. a. Incorrect.

    b. Correct.

Explanation: Place the amount of taxes as the part and total earnings as the whole, which provides the fraction 6,125/24,500 (reduced to 1/4). Since the fraction 1/4 is less than the fraction 1/3, the tax deductions amount is less than Calvin believed.

13. a. Incorrect. You chose the fraction that represents the increase.
    b. Correct.
    c. Incorrect. You used the number of sophomores as the part in the fraction.
    d. Incorrect.

   Explanation: The number of total students is computed by adding the number of freshmen and the number of sophomores (625 + 450 = 1,075). The number of freshmen represents the part and total students represents the whole, which provides the fraction 625/1,075 (reduced to 25/43).

14. a. Incorrect. You chose the fraction representing the amount of increase in applications.
    b. Incorrect. You used the difference between the number enrolling and the number applying as the part of the fraction.
    c. Incorrect. You followed the correct procedure but did not reduce the fraction to lowest terms.
    d. Correct.

   Explanation: The number of students who enrolled is the part and the number of students applying is the whole, which provides the fraction 650/800 (reduced to 13/16).

15. a. Incorrect. You used the hours worked by Thomas as the part and the hours worked by Lopez as the whole.
    b. Incorrect. You used the hours worked by Lopez as the part of the fraction.
    c. Correct.
    d. Incorrect. You followed the correct procedure but failed to reduce the fraction to lowest terms.

   Explanation: Total hours worked is found by adding the hours worked by each attorney (16 + 9 + 15 = 40). The hours worked by Henson is the part and the total hours worked is the whole, which provides the fraction 16/40 (reduced to 2/5).

16. a. Correct.
    b. Incorrect. You followed the correct procedure, but made an error in computation which moved the decimal point one place too far to the left.
    c. Incorrect. You divided by the fractional increase.
    d. Incorrect.

Explanation: The salary is multiplied by the fractional increase to find the salary increase amount ($21,300 x 1/10 = $2,130).

17. a. Correct.
    b. Incorrect.
    c. Incorrect.
    d. Incorrect.

Explanation: Find the total amount due by subtracting the discount amount from the original cost of the furniture.

18. a. Correct.
    b. Incorrect.

Explanation: Find the profit on the house by subtracting the cost of the house from the sale price ($147,500 – $121,100 = $26,400). Benson's profit is found by multiplying the profit amount by Benson's share of the profits ($26,400 x 1/4 = $6,600). Benson's $6,600 part of the profit was greater than his $6,500 goal.

19. a. Correct.
    b. Incorrect. You found the profit amount for Mario.
    c. Incorrect. You found the profit amount for Lewis.
    d. Incorrect. You chose the total profit amount.

Explanation: Art's profit is found by multiplying the total profit by the fractional share for Art's contribution ($62,000 x 2/5 = $24,800).

20. a. Correct.
    b. Incorrect. You found the amount due to the widow.
    c. Incorrect. You multiplied the number of acres of property by the share due to each child.
    d. Incorrect.

Explanation: The amount due for each child is found by multiplying the total property value by the fractional share due to each child (1/2 x 1/2 = 1/4; $184,400 x 1/4 = $46,100).

21. a. Incorrect.
    b. Incorrect.
    c. Correct.
    d. Incorrect.

Explanation: There are 12 months in a year, so multiply annual earnings by 1/12, then multiply the answer by 1/4.

22. a. Incorrect. You did not subtract the discount.
    b. Incorrect. You found only the discount amount.
    c. Correct.
    d. Incorrect. You added the discount amount to the original cost amount.

    Explanation: Find the discount amount by multiplying the original price by the discount fraction ($680 x 1/4 = $170). Then subtract the discount amount from the original price ($680 – $170 = $510).

23. a. Correct.
    b. Incorrect.

    Explanation: Find the number of questions that Deana answered correctly by subtracting the number missed from the number possible (240 – 33 = 207). The number of questions that must be answered correctly to pass can be found by multiplying the number possible by the fraction that must be answered correctly (240 x 4/5 = 192). Since Deana answered more than 192 questions correctly, she passed the test.

24. a. Incorrect. You multiplied by only the whole number part of the mixed fraction.
    b. Incorrect. You multiplied by only the fractional part of the mixed fraction.
    c. Correct.
    d. Incorrect.

    Explanation: Find the speed after completing the training by multiplying the original speed by the rate of increase (90 x 2 1/2 = 225).

25. a. Correct.
    b. Incorrect. You included only the whole number part of the mixed fractions for daily hours worked to find total hours worked.
    c. Incorrect. You multiplied the hourly pay rate by the number of hours worked only on Monday.
    d. Incorrect.

    Explanation: Add the number of hours worked each day (4 1/2 + 6 1/4 + 3 3/4 = 13 6/4 or 14 2/4; reduced to 14 1/2). Then, multiply the hours worked by the hourly pay rate (14 1/2 x $8.60 = $124.70).

SECTION 6: Decimals

1. a	10. a	19. a
2. b	11. a	20. a
3. b	12. d	21. a
4. d	13. a	22. a
5. b	14. d	23. b
6. a	15. c	24. a
7. b	16. a	25. c
8. a	17. b	
9. c	18. d	

Explanations

1. a

2. b

3. b

4. d

5. b

6. a. Correct.

   b. Incorrect.

   Explanation: The cost of a dozen pens from the mail order catalog is found by adding the cost of the pens and the shipping charges ($5.76 + $.60 = $6.36). The cost of a dozen pens from the local supplier is found by multiplying the cost per pen by 12—the number in a dozen ($.55 x 12 = $6.60). Therefore, the $6.36 amount computed for the mail order catalog is the lowest.

7. a. Incorrect. You found the cost per pad.

   b. Correct.

   c. Incorrect. You found the cost for 1 dozen.

   d. Incorrect. You found the number of pads that will be ordered.

   Explanation: The cost for 4 dozen is found by multiplying the cost per dozen by the number of dozens ordered ($6 x 4 = $24).

8. a. Correct.

   b. Incorrect. You added instead of multiplying.

   c. Incorrect. You subtracted instead of multiplying.

   d. Incorrect. You divided instead of multiplying.

Explanation: Find the total cost by multiplying the cost per chair by the number of chairs needed ($339.95 x 5 = $1,699.75).

9. a. Incorrect. You found only total deductions.
   b. Incorrect. You added total deductions to earnings.
   c. Correct.
   d. Incorrect.

Explanation: Find the total deductions by adding the individual amounts ($48.75 + $175.83 + $25.00 = $249.58). The paycheck amount is found by subtracting the total deduction amount from the earnings ($875.00 – $249.58 = $625.42).

10. a. Correct.
    b. Incorrect. You multiplied instead of dividing.
    c. Incorrect. You subtracted instead of dividing.
    d. Incorrect. You added instead of dividing.

Explanation: Find the number of shares that can be purchased by dividing the total amount available by the cost per share ($1,251.25 / $89.375 = 14).

11. a. Correct.
    b. Incorrect. You followed the correct procedure, but placed the decimal point two places too far to the right in your answer.
    c. Incorrect. You followed the correct procedure, but placed the decimal point one place too far to the right in your answer.
    d. Incorrect.

Explanation: The premium amount is found by multiplying the insured amount by the cost rate per dollar ($180,000 x $.00295 = $531).

12. a. Incorrect. You included the cost and shipping charge for only one disk.
    b. Incorrect. You found the cost of the order correctly, but subtracted the shipping charges.
    c. Incorrect. You found the cost of the disks correctly, but did not include the shipping charges.
    d. Correct.

Explanation: The cost of the disks is found by multiplying the cost per disk by the number of disks ($11.99 x 3 = $35.97). Shipping charges are found by adding the cost of shipping each of the three disks ($1.29 + $.42 + $.42 = $2.13). Then add the cost of the disks and the shipping costs ($35.97 + $2.13 = $38.10).

13. a. Correct.
   b. Incorrect. You found the amount needed to order only 9 items.
   c. Incorrect. You multiplied the cost per item by the number in each package and then multiplied by the number of items needed.
   d. Incorrect. You only included the number of items to be ordered expressed in dollars as your answer.

   Explanation: Since the product can be ordered only in packages containing 6 items, 12 items must be ordered to supply the 9 items needed. The cost of the order is found by multiplying the price per item by the number of items to order ($18 x 12 = $216).

14. a. Incorrect. You found the regular price correctly, but multiplied the sales price for a package by the number of sales in each group.
   b. Incorrect. You found the regular price without subtracting the promotional price.
   c. Incorrect. You found the promotional price without subtracting it from the regular price.
   d. Correct.

   Explanation: The regular price is found by multiplying the cost per tissue roll by the number of rolls ($1.45 x 12 = $17.40). The savings price is found by multiplying the price of 3 sale packages by the number of 3 packs in 12 ($4 x 4 = $16). To find total savings, subtract the savings price from the regular price ($17.40 − $16.00 = $1.40).

15. a. Incorrect. You multiplied the number of miles represented by each unit by the distance on the map (100 x 2.5 = 250).
   b. Incorrect. You multiplied the number of miles represented by each unit by the scale (100 x .5 = 50).
   c. Correct.
   d. Incorrect. You divided the number of miles represented by each unit by the unit (100 / .5 = 200).

   Explanation: Find the number of scale units by dividing the map distance by the map scale (2.5 / .5 = 5). To find the number of miles, multiply the number of scale units by the number of miles represented by each unit (5 x 100 = 500).

16. a. Correct.
   b. Incorrect.

   Explanation: The number of feet available is found by dividing the distance on the blueprint by the scale representing 1 foot (4.75 / .25 = 19). Since there are 20 feet of expansion space available, this space will be large enough.

17. a. Incorrect. You divided the number of weeks in each group by the rate of vacation days earned for each group (2 / .5 = 4).
    b. Correct.
    c. Incorrect. You divided the number of days in the year by the number of weeks in each group (52 / 2 = 26).
    d. Incorrect. You divided the number of weeks in a year by the rate of vacation days earned for each group (52 / .5 = 104).

    Explanation: First find the number of groups of 2 contained in 52 weeks (52 / 2 = 26). Then multiply by the number of vacation days for each group to compute the number of vacation days earned during the year (26 x .5 = 13).

18. a. Incorrect. You did not include shipping charges in your answer.
    b. Incorrect. You included shipping charges for each group of items instead of shipping charges for the order as a whole.
    c. Incorrect. You subtracted shipping charges.
    d. Correct.

    Explanation: The cost of each product is found by multiplying the price of each item by the number of items: Memo pads (184 x $.45 = $82.80); envelopes (50 x $.75 = $37.50); disks (8 x $14.95 = $119.60). The cost of the total order is found by adding the cost of each product and the shipping charges ($82.80 + $37.50 + $119.60 + $20 = $259.90).

19. a. Correct.
    b. Incorrect.

    Explanation: First find out how many boxes of folders are needed by dividing the total number needed by the number of folders in each box (400 / 50 = 8). Then multiply the cost of a box of folders by the number of boxes needed ($4.00 x 8 = $32.00). Since the order is only $32, the $35 that is available is enough to pay for the order.

20. a. Correct.
    b. Incorrect.

    Explanation: The cost of the order is found by multiplying the cost per roll by the number of rolls ordered ($5.85 x 90 = $526.50). The $568.65 budget is enough to cover this order amount.

21. a. Correct.
    b. Incorrect. You divided the number of rolls ordered by the cost per roll (200 / $.08 = $2,500).
    c. Incorrect. You multiplied the cost for 12 rolls by the number of rolls ordered ($.96 x 200 = $192).
    d. Incorrect.

Explanation: The cost of each roll is found by dividing the cost for 12 rolls by 12 ($.96 / 12 = $.08). The cost of the order is then found by multiplying the cost of each roll by the number of rolls ordered ($.08 x 200 = $16.00).

22. a. Correct.
    b. Incorrect. You included only the amount of the purchase.
    c. Incorrect. You added the amount of the purchase to the amount given to cover the cost of the snack.
    d. Incorrect.

Explanation: The cost of the snack is found by adding the cost of each item ($2.85 + $.75 = $3.60). The amount of change is found by subtracting the amount of the purchase from the amount of money given to Ken ($20.00 – $3.60 = $16.40).

23. a. Incorrect. You included only the total cost amount.
    b. Correct.
    c. Incorrect. You subtracted the cost for 1 case from the total cost ($127.50 – $25.50 = $102).
    d. Incorrect. You added the cost for 1 case to the total cost ($127.50 + $25.50 = $153).

Explanation: The refund amount for one case of paper is found by dividing the total cost by the number of cases ($127.50 / 5 = $25.50).

24. a. Correct.
    b. Incorrect.
    c. Incorrect.
    d. Incorrect.

Explanation: First find the cost of each box of pens by dividing the total cost by the number of boxes purchased. Then, find the refund amount by multiplying the cost of each box by the number of boxes returned.

25. a. Incorrect. You included only the four chairs and left off the other items.
    b. Incorrect. You included only one chair.
    c. Correct.
    d. Incorrect.

Explanation: The total cost is computed by adding the total of each item damaged ($56 + $22.50 + $1,359.80 + $60 = $1,498.30). Notice that there were four chairs for a total damage of $1,359.80 (4 x $339.95).

SECTION 7: Percents

Quick Check

1. c	10. b	19. b
2. b	11. b	20. b
3. a	12. d	21. c
4. c	13. d	22. c
5. b	14. d	23. b
6. a	15. a	24. c
7. b	16. d	25. d
8. b	17. a	
9. b	18. d	

Explanations

1. c

2. b

3. a

4. c

5. b

6. a. Correct.
   b. Incorrect.

   Explanation: Divide Hal's current rent by his monthly income (600 / 1600 = .375). Move the decimal point two places to the left to find that Hal is paying 37.5 percent of his salary in rent.

7. a. Incorrect.
   b. Correct.
   c. Incorrect.
   d. Incorrect.

   Explanation: Convert the percentage by moving the decimal point two places to the left and then multiply by the total balance (.025 x $922.40 = $23.06).

8. a. Incorrect.
   b. Correct.

   Explanation: Divide the number of employees eligible for retirement by the total number of employees. Note that the answer is converted to a percent by moving the decimal point two places to the right. This value (25 percent) is less than the 30 percent goal.

9. a. Incorrect.
   b. Correct.

   Explanation: The rate of absenteeism is found by dividing the number of days absent by the total working days (24 / 480 = .05 or 5 percent). The rate is lower.

10. a. Incorrect. You found the percent for a category that was not requested.
    b. Correct.
    c. Incorrect. You found the percent correctly, but added it to 100.
    d. Incorrect.

    Explanation: The first step is to find the total amount overdue ($40,000 + $20,000 + $20,000 = $80,000). The percent represented by the debts 90 days or more overdue is found by dividing the amount overdue in this category by the total amount overdue (20,000 / 80,000 = 0.25 or 25 percent).

11. a. Incorrect. You followed the correct procedure, but placed the decimal point one place too far to the left in your answer.
    b. Correct.
    c. Incorrect. You followed the correct procedure, but did not move the decimal point two places to the right to convert the decimal to a percent.
    d. Incorrect. You found the percent of expenses that did not relate to salaries.

    Explanation: The percent of expenses used on salaries is found by dividing the salaries by the total expenses ($117,000 / $180,000 = 0.65 or 65 percent).

12. a. Incorrect. You found the percent of expenses that do not relate to supplies.
    b. Incorrect. You followed the correct procedure, but placed the decimal point one place too far to the right in your answer.
    c. Incorrect. You followed the correct procedure, but placed the decimal point one place too far to the left in your answer.
    d. Correct.

    Explanation: The first step is to find the total expenses ($128,000 + $12,800 + $19,200 = $160,000). The percent of expenses for supplies is then found by dividing the supplies amount by the total expense amount ($12,800 / $160,000 = 0.08 or 8 percent).

13. a. Incorrect.
    b. Incorrect.
    c. Incorrect.
    d. Correct.

Explanation: More information is needed to determine if this is an acceptable level.

14. a. Incorrect. You used the number remaining in stock as the percent used.
  b. Incorrect. You found the percent remaining in stock.
  c. Incorrect. You used the number of cartridges used as the percent used.
  d. Correct.

Explanation: Find the number of toners used by subtracting the number remaining from the number available (120 − 72 = 48). Find the percent of toners used by dividing the number used by the number available (48 / 120 = 0.4 or 40 percent).

15. a. Correct.
  b. Incorrect. You followed the correct procedure, but placed the decimal point one place too far to the right in your answer.
  c. Incorrect. You followed the correct procedure, but placed the decimal point one place too far to the left in your answer.
  d. Incorrect.

Explanation: The first step is to find the total amount of sales during the week ($1,198 + $1,231 + $1,210 + $1,317 + $1,476 + $1,568 = $8,000). The percent made on Saturday is then computed by dividing the sales on Saturday by the total sales ($1,568 / $8,000 = .196 or 19.6 percent).

16. a. Incorrect. You followed the correct procedure, but placed the decimal point one place too far to the left in your answer.
  b. Incorrect. You divided the weekly earnings by the savings rate.
  c. Incorrect. You subtracted the savings rate from the weekly earnings.
  d. Correct.

Explanation: The savings fund amount is found by multiplying the weekly earnings by the savings rate ($465.80 x .05 = $23.29).

17. a. Correct.
  b. Incorrect.

Explanation: The amount of the raise is found by multiplying the annual earnings by the 6 percent raise ($28,540.50 x .06 = $1,712.43). This amount is higher than the $1,700 expectation.

18. a. Incorrect. You found only the annual raise amount.
  b. Incorrect. You divided the annual salary by 12.
  c. Incorrect. You may have found the correct raise amount, but divided the raise amount by 10.
  d. Correct.

Explanation: First find the annual raise by multiplying the annual salary by the raise percent ($36,000 x .08 = $2,880). The amount of the monthly raise is then found by dividing the annual raise amount by 12 because there are 12 months in the year ($2,880 / 12 = $240).

19. a. Incorrect. You only found the raise amount.

   b. Correct.

   c. Incorrect. You subtracted the raise amount from the previous salary.

   d. Incorrect. You included the previous salary, without a raise.

Explanation: Multiply the annual salary by the raise percent ($34,600 x .075 = $2,595). Then add the raise amount to the previous salary ($34,600 + $2,595 = $37,195).

20. a. Incorrect.

   b. Correct.

Explanation: Divide the raise amount by the salary amount ($52.20 / $580 = .09 or 9 percent). This percent is higher than the 8 percent raise awarded last year.

21. a. Incorrect. You followed the correct procedure, but then subtracted the percent from 100.

   b. Incorrect. You followed the correct procedure, but placed the decimal point one place too far to the right in your answer.

   c. Correct.

   d. Incorrect. You followed the correct procedure, but did not move the decimal point two places to the right to convert the value to a percent.

Explanation: The raise amount is found by subtracting last year's salary from this year's salary ($23,760 – $22,000 = $1,760). The raise percent is found by dividing the raise amount by last year's salary ($1,760 / $22,000 = .08; or 8 percent).

22. a. Incorrect. You followed the correct procedure, but did not move the decimal point two places to the right to convert the decimal value to a percent.

   b. Incorrect. You followed the correct procedure, but placed the decimal point one place too far to the left in your answer.

   c. Correct.

   d. Incorrect. You followed the correct procedure, but placed the decimal point one place too far to the right in your answer.

Explanation: The commission percent is found by dividing the commission amount by the sales amount ($108.25 / $8,660 = .0125 or 1.25 percent).

23. a. Incorrect. You found only the amount to be added to the cost of the book.
    b. Correct.
    c. Incorrect. You subtracted the amount to be added from the cost of the book.
    d. Incorrect. You chose the cost of the book without including the amount to be added to determine the sales price.

    Explanation: Multiply the cost of the book by the increase percent ($22.50 x .22 = $4.95). The price of the book is then found by adding the increase to the cost of the book ($22.50 + $4.95 = $27.45).

24. a. Incorrect. You included only the raise amount.
    b. Incorrect. You subtracted the raise amount from current earnings.
    c. Correct.
    d. Incorrect. You followed the correct procedure, but used the decimal value .625 instead of .0625 to compute the raise amount.

    Explanation: Find the raise amount by multiplying the current earnings by the raise percent ($26,800 x .0625 = $1,675). The new salary is then found by adding the raise amount to the current earnings ($26,800 + $1,675 = $28,475).

25. a. Incorrect.
    b. Incorrect.
    c. Incorrect.
    d. Correct.

    Explanation: The minimum payment is found by multiplying the account balance by the minimum payment percent ($5,000 x .10 = $500). Then, find the additional amount due by subtracting the actual payment from the minimum payment ($500 − $300 = $200).

SECTION 8: Ratios and Proportions

1. b	10. a	19. a
2. c	11. b	20. a
3. b	12. b	21. c
4. b	13. b	22. a
5. a	14. d	23. a
6. d	15. a	24. a
7. a	16. a	25. b
8. b	17. a	
9. c	18. c	

Explanations

1. b

2. c

3. b

4. b

5. a

6. a. Incorrect. You used the time, 60 days ago, while making the comparison.

   b. Incorrect. You used the time, an incorrect number, to represent the instructors.

   c. Incorrect. You followed the correct procedure, but did not reduce to lowest terms.

   d. Correct.

   Explanation: The ratio of 30 marketing representatives to 2 instructors is expressed as 30:2, which is reduced to 15:1.

7. a. Correct.

   b. Incorrect. This alternative will produce an invalid ratio of 6:1.

   c. Incorrect. This alternative will produce an invalid ratio of 30:1.

   d. Incorrect.

   Explanation: The ratio of marketing representatives to the number who reached their quotas is found by comparing the number in each category as indicated in a ratio (30:6, reduced to 5:1).

8. a. Incorrect. You expressed the ratio by comparing the number who are furnished cars to 1.

   b. Correct.

   c. Incorrect. You found the appropriate ratio, but reversed the factors—16:48 instead of 48:16.

   d. Incorrect. You followed the correct procedure, but did not reduce the ratio to lowest terms.

   Explanation: The ratio is found by comparing the number of marketing representatives and managers to the 16 who are furnished cars (48:16, reduced to 3:1).

9. a. Incorrect. You compared the number of states (18) to the number of marketing representatives (4).

   b. Incorrect. You expressed the total sales volume compared to the value 1 as a ratio.

   c. Correct.

   d. Incorrect. You followed the correct procedure, but did not reduce the ratio to lowest terms.

   Explanation: Find the total sales by adding the number of sales (12 + 8 + 24 + 4 = 48). The ratio of the 48 sales to the 4 marketing representatives is 48:4, reduced to 12: 1.

10. a. Correct.

    b. Incorrect.

    Explanation: The ratio of the 150 words to the 3 minutes timed on the test is expressed as 150:3, reduced to 50:1. This ratio is above the minimum needed to pass the test.

11. a. Incorrect. You compared the number of boxes to the value 1.

    b. Correct.

    c. Incorrect. You compared the number of boxes to the number of shipping clerks.

    d. Incorrect.

    Explanation: The ratio of the 180 reams of paper to the 15 boxes is 180:15, reduced to 12:1.

12. a. Incorrect. You used the ratio for only last month.

    b. Correct.

    c. Incorrect. You used the number of new boats compared to the value 1 in your ratio.

    d. Incorrect.

Explanation: First find the number of new boats (16 + 26 = 42) and the number of used boats (8 + 6 = 14) sold during the 2-month period. The ratio is 42:14, reduced to 3:1.

13. a. Incorrect.

    b. Correct.

Explanation: The ratio of 234 days present to 18 days absent is 234:18, reduced to 13:1. This ratio is less than the 15:1 acceptable ratio.

14. a. Incorrect. You compared the number of employees on the first assembly line to the total number of supervisors.

    b. Incorrect. You compared the number of assembly lines to the value 1.

    c. Incorrect. You compared the total number of assembly line employees to the value 1.

    d. Correct.

Explanation: Add the number of employees on the assembly lines (8 + 10 + 10 = 28). The ratio of the 28 employees on the assembly line to the 4 supervisors is expressed as 28:4, reduced to 7:1.

15. a. Correct.

    b. Incorrect.

Explanation: First find the total number of patients (105 + 89 + 112 = 306). The ratio of the 306 patients to the 3 dentists is 306:3, reduced to 102:1. This ratio is less than the 105:1 ratio of Dr. Holt.

16. a. Correct.

    b. Incorrect. You related boxes to price, but reversed the ratio.

    c. Incorrect. You related price to boxes and boxes to price.

    d. Incorrect.

Explanation: The relation of boxes to price (5/$3) can be applied to determine the price of the purchase for 45 boxes 45/$? (5/$3:45/$?).

17. a. Correct.

    b. Incorrect.

Explanation: Compare the relationship of 3 machines to 28 meters, to the relationship of 12 machines to an unknown amount of space (3/28:12/?). Calculation shows 3 x ? = 336; 112 is the unknown amount. Therefore, the 118 square meters is enough.

18. a. Incorrect. You found the number of items produced by each employee.

    b. Incorrect. You incorrectly set the proportion as 18/72:140/?.

    c. Correct.

    d. Incorrect.

    Explanation: Compare 18 employees producing 72 items to an unknown number of employees producing 140 items (18/72:?/140. This proportion gives a value of 35 (72 x ? = 2,520 or ? = 35).

19. a. Correct.

    b. Incorrect.

    Explanation: Compare 17 sheets to cover 238 square feet and 25 sheets to cover an unknown area with the following proportion: 17/238:25/?. This provides a value of 350 (17 x ? = 5,950 or ? = 350). There are more than enough sheets of plywood to cover the 322 square feet.

20. a. Correct.

    b. Incorrect. You completed the correct calculation, but divided the answer by 2.

    c. Incorrect. You used an incorrect proportion 2/$37:$370/?.

    d. Incorrect.

    Explanation: The relationship of 2 shirts for $37 and an unknown number of shirts for $370 is 2/$37:?/$370. This proportion provides a value of 20 as the unknown number.

21. a. Incorrect. You found the number of cans per error.

    b. Incorrect. You multiplied the number of errors currently (15) by 90.

    c. Correct.

    d. Incorrect.

    Explanation: The relationship between 15 mistakes for 7,500 cans processed and 90 mistakes for an unknown number of cans processed is 15/7,500:90/?. This proportion provides a value of 45,000 (15 x ? = 675,000 or ? = 45,000).

22. a. Correct.

    b. Incorrect.

    Explanation: The relationship between 90 people touring in 1.5 hours and an unknown number of people touring in 9 hours is 90/1.5:?/9. This proportion provides a value of 540 (1.5 = 810 or ? = 540). This number is greater than the specified 500 people to tour during the 9 hours.

23. a. Correct.
    b. Incorrect.
    c. Incorrect.
    d. Incorrect.

Explanation: The relationship between 400 gallons of gasoline being used to drive 6,000 miles and an unknown number of gallons of gasoline needed to drive 84,000 miles is 400/6,000:?/84,000. This proportion provides a value of 5,600 gallons (6,000 x ? = 33,600,000 or ? = 5,600). This number of gallons is greater than the 5,000 gallons included in the alternatives.

24. a. Correct.
    b. Incorrect. You multiplied the amount paid by the percent ($840 x .80).
    c. Incorrect. You multiplied the amount paid by the percent and then added this amount to the amount paid ($840 x .80 = $672 + $840 = $1,512).
    d. Incorrect.

Explanation: The relationship between 80 percent, representing the $840 paid on the bill, and 100 percent, representing an unknown total amount of the bill, is 80/$840:100/?. This proportion provides a value of $1,050 (80 x ? = $84,000 or ? = $1,050).

25. a. Incorrect.
    b. Correct.

Explanation: The maximum amount of the monthly income that should be allocated to mortgage payments is found by multiplying the monthly income by 25 percent ($4,000 x .25 = $1,000). Therefore, the client's monthly income supports a $1,000 monthly mortgage payment—not the $1,200 payment being made.

SECTION 9: Combination Problems

Quick Check

1. a	10. d	19. b
2. d	11. c	20. a
3. b	12. a	21. d
4. a	13. c	22. c
5. b	14. a	23. b
6. c	15. a	24. c
7. a	16. a	25. b
8. d	17. b	
9. b	18. a	

Explanations

1. a
2. d
3. b
4. a
5. b
6. a. Incorrect. You placed the number of males as the part and the number of females as the whole.
   b. Incorrect. You followed the correct procedure, but did not reduce the fraction to lowest terms.
   c. Correct.
   d. Incorrect. You placed the number of males as the part and the number of females as the whole and then reduced the fraction to lowest terms.

   Explanation: There are 3 males out of 9 employees. Males represent the part and total employees represents the whole. This is stated as the fraction 3/9, reduced to 1/3.

7. a. Correct.
   b. Incorrect. You used 3 weeks as the part and the number of computers in repair for 3 weeks or longer as the whole.
   c. Incorrect. You used the number of computers in need of repair for 3 weeks or longer as the part and the number needing repair last year as the whole.
   d. Incorrect.

   Explanation: The number of computers needing repair represents the part. The total number of computers represents the whole. This is stated as the fraction 14/70, reduced to 1/5.

8. a. Incorrect. You used 300 as the part and $12,000 as the whole, then reduced to lowest terms.

   b. Incorrect. You multiplied the sales figure by the fractional value.

   c. Incorrect. You followed much of the correct procedure, but then made the value 1 the part and the number of products with sales in excess of $12,000 as the whole to form a fraction.

   d. Correct.

   Explanation: Multiply the number of total parts by the fractional value representing the number in excess of $12,000 (300 x 1/6 = 50).

9. a. Correct.

   b. Incorrect.

   Explanation: Multiply the total rental fee by the fractional part desired by Byte ($72,000 x 1/24 = $3,000). This amount does not exceed the cost budgeted.

10. a. Incorrect. You selected the alternative that represents the total bill earned by all partners.

    b. Incorrect. You divided the total bill by the number of hours spent by Cole.

    c. Incorrect. You divided the total bill by the fractional part of the time Cole spent on the case.

    d. Correct.

    Explanation: First find the total number of hours worked on the case (6 + 5 + 4 = 15). The part of the total time spent by Cole is the part and total hours is the whole (5/15, reduced to 1/3). Then multiply the total bill by the fractional part of the time Cole spent on the case ($4,800 x 1/3 = $1,600).

11. a. Incorrect. You found the total of the two discounts.

    b. Incorrect. You found the total of the two items without subtracting the discounts.

    c. Correct.

    d. Incorrect. You added the discounts to the original list prices of the two items.

    Explanation: The discounts on the two items are first found as follows: Chair—$50 ($250 x 1/5 = $50) and Sofa—$125 ($500 x 1/4 = $125). The amount to be paid is then found by subtracting the discounts from the list price for each item ($250 – $50 = $200); and ($500 – $125 = $375). The final charge to the customer is found by adding the prices of the two items after subtracting discounts, $575 ($200 + $375 = $575).

12. a. Correct.
    b. Incorrect. You divided the total number of pens ordered by the cost per pen.
    c. Incorrect. You divided the total number of pens to be ordered by the cost for 12 pens.
    d. Incorrect.

    Explanation: First divide the cost of 12 pens by the value 12 to find the cost per pen ($7.20 / 12 = $0.60). The cost of the order is then found by multiplying the total number of pens ordered by the cost per pen (360 x $0.60 = $216).

13. a. Incorrect. You subtracted a $1.50 shipping charge for the entire order.
    b. Incorrect. You added a $1.50 shipping charge for the complete order instead of for each disk.
    c. Correct.
    d. Incorrect.

    Explanation: The total cost for each disk is found by adding the price of the disk to the shipping charges ($12 + $1.50 = $13.50). Then multiply the total cost for each disk by the number of disks ordered ($13.50 x 20 = $270) to find the cost of the order.

14. a. Correct.
    b. Incorrect.

    Explanation: The number of covers needed for 4 weeks is found by multiplying the number used each week by 4 (30 x 4 = 120). The cost per cover from Direct Mail Plus is found by dividing the cost for 12 covers by 12 ($6.60 / 12 = $.55). Then multiply the number needed by the cost per cover, plus shipping charges (120 x $.55 = $66; then, $66 + $10 = $76). The cost of the order from The Supply Shop is found by multiplying the number needed by the cost per cover (120 x $.66 = $79.20). Direct Mail Plus offers the lowest price.

15. a. Correct.
    b. Incorrect. You did not include shipping charges.
    c. Incorrect. You subtracted shipping charges.
    d. Incorrect.

    Explanation: Multiply the unit price by the number of items as follows: Blush brushes, 180 x $.35 = $63; cotton balls, 70 x $.80 = $56; and concealer, 6 x $14.95 = $89.70. The total cost of the order is then found by adding the total cost of each item and the shipping charge ($63 + $56 + $89.70 + $25 = $233.70).

16. a. Correct.
    b. Incorrect.

    Explanation: Divide the total cost by the number of items ($55.50 / 150 = $.37). Then multiply by the number of items returned. This is the amount of the refund.

17. a. Incorrect. You found the percent relating to expenses other than salaries.
    b. Correct.
    c. Incorrect. You found the percent relating to expenses other than salaries. Another error was to place the decimal point one place too far to the left in the answer.
    d. Incorrect. You followed the correct procedure, but placed the decimal point one place too far to the left in the answer.

    Explanation: First find the total ($134,850 + $21,000 + $18,150 = $174,000). The percent of total expenses for salaries is found by dividing the salaries amount by the total expense amount ($134,850 / $174,000 = .775 or 77.5 percent).

18. a. Correct.
    b. Incorrect.
    c. Incorrect.
    d. Incorrect.

    Explanation: Multiply the weekly salary by the percent deduction ($525 x .06 = $31.50). This amount exceeds the $30 savings goal.

19. a. Incorrect.
    b. Correct.
    c. Incorrect.
    d. Incorrect.

    Explanation: The raise amount is found by multiplying his annual salary by the raise percent ($42,000 x .065 = $2,730). Then add the raise amount to the previous salary ($42,000 + $2,730 = $44,730).

20. a. Correct.
    b. Incorrect.
    c. Incorrect.
    d. Incorrect.

    Explanation: The commission rate is found by dividing the commission amount by the sales amount ($483 / $4,600 = .105. The decimal point is then moved two places to the right to convert the rate to a percent (.105 = 10.5 percent).

21. a. Incorrect. You included only the amount paid.
    b. Incorrect. You followed the correct procedure, but left off a zero in the answer.
    c. Incorrect. You multiplied the amount paid by the percent of the whole amount it represents.
    d. Correct.

    Explanation: The relationship between 5 percent, representing $400, and 100 percent, representing an unknown amount, is expressed as: 5/$400:100/?. This proportion provides a value of $8,000 (5 x ? = $40,000 or ? = $8,000).

22. a. Incorrect. You related the number of courses to the value 1.
    b. Incorrect. You related the number of faculty members to the value 1.
    c. Correct.
    d. Incorrect. You related the number of students to the value 1.

    Explanation: The relationship between 1,600 students to 20 faculty members is expressed with the following ratio: 1,600:20 reduced to 80:1.

23. a. Incorrect.
    b. Correct.

    Explanation: The relationship between the 800 employees and the 25 who were absent is expressed with the following ratio: 800:25 reduced to 32:1. This is less than the 35:1 acceptable ratio.

24. a. Incorrect. You multiplied the number of boxes to be ordered by the cost of 5 boxes.
    b. Incorrect. You multiplied the cost for 5 boxes by the value 5.
    c. Correct.
    d. Incorrect. You established an incorrect proportion as follows: 5/3:?/40.

    Explanation: The relationship between 5 boxes costing $3 and 40 boxes costing an unknown amount is: 5/$3:40/?. This proportion provides the value of $24 (5 x ? = $120 or ? = $24).

25. a. Incorrect. You chose the number required to cover 3,000 square feet of roof.
    b. Correct.
    c. Incorrect. You divided by the number of packs needed to cover a 3,000 square foot roof.
    d. Incorrect. You divided the number of square feet in the new house by the number of packs of shingles needed to cover the previous house.

    Explanation: The relationship between 30 packs to cover 3,000 square feet and an unknown number of packs to cover 5,400 square feet is: 30/3,000:?/5,400. This proportion provides the value of 54 (3,000 x ? = 162,000 or ? = 54).

SECTION 10: Time

1. b	10. a	19. a
2. d	11. c	20. b
3. b	12. b	21. d
4. c	13. a	22. c
5. a	14. d	23. a
6. d	15. a	24. a
7. c	16. b	25. c
8. c	17. d	
9. b	18. a	

Explanations

Note the following conversion factors that will be useful for this section:

60 seconds	=	1 minute
60 minutes	=	1 hour
24 hours	=	1 day
7 days	=	1 week
365 days	=	1 year
52 weeks	=	1 year
12 months	=	1 year

All answers should be converted to the highest form. For example, 90 minutes will be converted to 1 hour, 30 minutes.

1. b
2. d
3. b
4. c
5. a
6. a. Incorrect. You added only the hour portions of the times.
   b. Incorrect. You added only the minute portions of the times.
   c. Incorrect. You may have followed the correct procedure, but made an error while converting the minute portions of the times.
   d. Correct.
   Explanation: Add the hours worked each day to find the total hours worked (5 1/2 + 6 3/4 = 12 1/4).

7. a. Incorrect. You subtracted the hours worked on Tuesday from the hours worked on Thursday.

   b. Incorrect. You probably followed the correct procedure, but made an error while converting minutes into hours.

   c. Correct.

   d. Incorrect. You added only the hour portions of the times.

   Explanation: Add the hours worked during each of the two days to find the total hours worked (5 3/4 + 7 3/4 = 13 1/2).

8. a. Incorrect. You divided the number of weeks by the number of applicants.

   b. Incorrect. You multiplied the number of weeks by the number of applicants.

   c. Correct.

   d. Incorrect. You multiplied the number of weeks by the day of the month.

   Explanation: Total days are found by multiplying the number of days in a week by the number of weeks (7 x 6 = 42).

9. a. Incorrect. You probably followed the correct procedure, but made an error while converting minutes into hours.

   b. Correct.

   c. Incorrect. You did not include the minute portions while determining the total hours.

   d. Incorrect. You included only the minute portion while determining the total hours.

   Explanation: Total hours worked is found by adding the number of hours worked during each of the two days (6 3/4 + 5 1/2 = 12 1/4).

10. a. Correct.

   b. Incorrect. You probably followed the correct procedure, but made an error while converting minutes to hours.

   c. Incorrect. You included only the hour portions of the times in your computation.

   d. Incorrect. You included only the minute portions of the times in your computation.

   Explanation: Total hours worked is found by adding the number of hours worked on Monday to the number of hours worked on Tuesday (8 1/4 + 9 1/2 = 17 3/4).

11. a. Incorrect. You included only the hour portions of the times.

   b. Incorrect. You probably followed the correct procedure, but made an error while converting minutes to hours.

   c. Correct.

   d. Incorrect. You probably followed the correct procedure, but made an error while converting minutes to hours.

Explanation: Total hours spent on the lessons is found by adding the hours spent on lessons during each of the three days (3 1/4 + 2 1/2 + 2 3/4 = 8 1/2).

12. a. Incorrect. You included only the hours portion of the times.

    b. Correct.

    c. Incorrect. You probably followed the correct procedure, but made an error while converting minutes to hours.

    d. Incorrect. You determined the total hours worked correctly, but then added the required hours to work each week to this value.

Explanation: Total hours to be paid is found by adding the hours worked during each of the three days (6 1/2 + 5 3/4 + 8 = 20 1/4).

13. a. Correct.

    b. Incorrect.

Explanation: The earnings under the monthly plan are found by multiplying the number of months in a year by the monthly earnings, then adding the bonus amount (12 x $1,500 = $18,000; $18,000 + $500 = $18,500). The earnings under the weekly plan are found by multiplying the number of weeks in a year by the weekly earnings (52 x $300 = $15,600). The monthly plan results in higher earnings.

14. a. Incorrect. You did not subtract the hours that she did not work during the week.

    b. Incorrect. You added the hours that she did not work to 40, instead of subtracting them.

    c. Incorrect. You subtracted the whole hours and did not consider the portion of an hour that she left early while determining hours worked.

    d. Correct.

Explanation: Multiply the number of hours worked in a normal day by the number of days (8 x 5 = 40) to get the hours worked in a normal week. Then, find the hours actually worked by subtracting the hours missed (40 − 3 1/2 = 36 1/2).

15. a. Correct.

    b. Incorrect. You did not include the hours worked on Saturday.

    c. Incorrect. You did not include the fractional portion of an hour worked on Saturday while determining the total hours worked.

    d. Incorrect. You subtracted the hours worked on Saturday.

Explanation: Total hours worked during the normal week is found by multiplying the number of days by the number of hours worked each day (5 x 8 = 40). Then add the hours worked on Saturday to find total hours worked during the week (40 + 3 3/4 = 43 3/4).

16. a. Incorrect. You subtracted only the hour portion of the time each day to find the hours worked for that day.
    b. Correct.
    c. Incorrect. You probably followed the correct procedure, but made an error while converting minutes to hours.
    d. Incorrect. You probably followed the correct procedure, but made an error while converting minutes to hours.

    Explanation: Total hours worked is found by adding the hours worked during each of the two days (3 1/2 + 3 3/4 = 7 1/4).

17. a. Incorrect. You multiplied the normal number of hours worked each day by the number of days worked, without considering that Nancy worked late one day and left early on another day.
    b. Incorrect. You included the extra time worked on Tuesday, but did not consider the time missed due to leaving early on Friday.
    c. Incorrect. You subtracted the hours missed due to leaving early on Friday, but did not consider the extra time worked on Tuesday.
    d. Correct.

    Explanation: Total hours worked is found by adding the number of hours worked each day (8 + 8 1/2 + 8 + 8 + 6 1/4 = 38 3/4).

18. a. Correct.
    b. Incorrect.

    Explanation: The number of characters entered by Randy Hall is found by multiplying the number of characters per minute by the number of minutes in an hour (180 x 60 = 10,800). This value is higher than the 10,000 characters keyboarded by Bernie Smith.

19. a. Correct.
    b. Incorrect. You included the number of minutes in an hour.
    c. Incorrect. You included the total number of minutes allocated for the entire exam.
    d. Incorrect.

    Explanation: First, find the total number of minutes included in 1 1/2 hours by multiplying the number of minutes in an hour by 1 1/2 (60 x 1 1/2 = 90). Then, find the number of minutes for each part by dividing the number of minutes by the number of parts (90 / 6 = 15).

20. a. Incorrect. You rounded to the next number of even years.
    b. Correct.
    c. Incorrect. You included the number of months in a year as your answer.
    d. Incorrect. You rounded down to the number of whole years allowed to pay for the car.

Explanation: The number of years needed to pay the loan is found by dividing the total number of payment months by the number of months in a year (42 / 12 = 3 1/2).

21. a. Incorrect.
    b. Incorrect.
    c. Incorrect.
    d. Correct.

Explanation: Find the total payments for each plan as follows: Plan A: $100 x 52 x 3 = $15,600; Plan B: $425 x 12 x 3 = $15,300; Plan C: $200 x 26 x 3 = $15,600; Plan D: $900 x 6 x 3 = $16,200. Plan D will result in the highest total payments.

22. a. Incorrect. You divided by 10.
    b. Incorrect. You may have followed the correct procedure, but made an error in computation.
    c. Correct.
    d. Incorrect.

Explanation: The number of years remaining is found by dividing the number of months before retirement by the number of months in a year (72 / 12 = 6).

23. a. Correct.
    b. Incorrect.

Explanation: Total hours worked is found by adding the hours worked each day (5 1/2 + 6 3/4 + 7 3/4 + 8 = 28). Therefore, 28 hours exceeds the 27 hour per week legal limit.

24. a. Correct.
    b. Incorrect. You made an error while determining the last date by making the date 1 day too many.
    c. Incorrect. You made an error while determining the last date by making the date 2 days too many.
    d. Incorrect. You made an error while determining the last date by making the date 3 days too many.

Explanation: The number of days included in the three months needed to reach 60 days will be used to determine the last date (October, 8 + November, 30 + December, 22 = 60).

25. a. Incorrect. You included number of weeks of vacation.
    b. Incorrect. You divided the number of weeks in a year by the number of weeks of vacation.
    c. Correct.
    d. Incorrect. You added the number of weeks of vacation to the number of weeks in a year.

Explanation: Subtract the number of weeks of vacation from the total number of weeks in a year (52 − 3 = 49).

SECTION 11: Length

Quick Check

1. c	10. b	19. a
2. c	11. d	20. c
3. c	12. a	21. a
4. b	13. a	22. b
5. c	14. a	23. a
6. a	15. b	24. a
7. b	16. a	25. c
8. b	17. a	
9. b	18. b	

Explanations

Note the following conversion factors that will be useful for this section:

12 inches	=	1 foot
36 inches	=	1 yard
3 feet	=	1 yard
5,280 feet	=	1 mile
1,760 yards	=	1 mile

All answers should be converted to the highest form. For example, 16 inches will be converted to 1 foot, 4 inches.

1. c
2. c
3. c
4. b
5. c
6. a. Correct.
   b. Incorrect.

   Explanation: Multiply the number of measured feet by the number of inches per foot (6 x 12 = 72). Add the space needed by the various items (26 + 9 + 36 = 71). The space available is greater than the space needed.

7. a. Incorrect. You may have made an error in computation or conversion.

    b. Correct.

    c. Incorrect. You may have made an error in computation or conversion.

    d. Incorrect.

    Explanation: Convert the space available from feet to inches; then add the inches to determine the total space available (7 x 12 = 84; then, 84 + 6 = 90). The number of bookcases that will fit is found by dividing the space available by the space required for each bookcase (90 / 30 = 3).

8. a. Incorrect.

    b. Correct.

    Explanation: First convert the yards of cable available to feet (20 x 3 = 60). The cable needed is found by adding the requirements for the two printers (23 + 40 = 63). The available cable is not enough for the job.

9. a. Incorrect. You included the conversion of 3 feet per yard.

    b. Correct.

    c. Incorrect. You multiplied the distance by the conversion factor.

    d. Incorrect. You added the conversion factor to the distance.

    Explanation: The distance stated in feet is divided by 3 to convert to yards (48 / 3 = 16).

10. a. Incorrect.

    b. Correct.

    Explanation: The first step is to convert the yards to inches (5 x 36 = 180). The second step is to convert the feet to inches (2 x 12 = 24). The sum of these two values provides the shelf space in inches (180 + 24 = 204). The shelf space is divided by the space required for each box to determine the number of boxes that will fit on the shelf, 204 / 27 = 7 (rounded down). Only 7 of the 15 boxes will fit on the shelf.

11. a. Incorrect. You added the number of inches on the page to the number of spaces per inch.

    b. Incorrect. You subtracted the number of inches from the number of spaces per inch.

    c. Incorrect. You multiplied the number of spaces per inch by only the whole number portion of the fraction.

    d. Correct.

    Explanation: The number of spaces is found by multiplying the number of spaces per inch by the number of inches (12 x 9 1/2 = 114).

12. a. Correct.
    b. Incorrect. You may have made an error while converting feet to inches.
    c. Incorrect. You may have made an error during the conversion process.
    d. Incorrect. You may have made an error during the conversion process.

    Explanation: First convert the number of feet to inches (3 x 12 = 36). Then add the inches to the measurement (36 + 4 = 40). Since the door opening is 41 inches, the desk will fit through the door.

13. a. Correct.
    b. Incorrect.

    Explanation: The maximum number of inches that can be inked is found by multiplying the number of feet by the number of inches per foot (12 x 12 = 144). Since the ribbons are only 140 inches, they can be inked.

14. a. Correct.
    b. Incorrect.

    Explanation: The total yards needed is found by multiplying the yards needed for each uniform by the number of uniforms needed (4 2/3 x 6 = 28). The 30 yards of cloth in 1 bolt is enough.

15. a. Incorrect. You chose the size of each roll of linoleum.
    b. Correct.
    c. Incorrect. You subtracted the size of each roll of linoleum from the floor size.
    d. Incorrect. You added the size of each roll of linoleum to the roof size.

    Explanation: The number of rolls needed is found by dividing the floor size by the size of each roll of linoleum (1,248 / 32 = 39).

16. a. Correct.
    b. Incorrect.

    Explanation: The size of the rug is first converted to feet (4 x 3 = 12 and 2 x 3 = 6). Therefore, the rug size of 12 feet by 6 feet will fit into the office space.

17. a. Correct.
    b. Incorrect.

    Explanation: The border length is found by multiplying the number of yards by 3 to convert yards to feet (59 x 3 = 177). Therefore, the border length is sufficient for the length of the 165-foot hallway.

18. a. Incorrect.

b. Correct.

Explanation: The available cabling in inches is found by multiplying the number of yards by 36 to convert yards to inches (40 x 36 = 1,440). The cable needed is found by multiplying the number of computers by the inches of cable needed for each one (36 x 45 = 1,620). George needs more cable than he has.

19. a. Correct.

b. Incorrect. You found only the number of total yards needed.

c. Incorrect. You divided by the conversion factor of 3.

d. Incorrect.

Explanation: Total yards is found by multiplying the number of rolls by the number of yards in each roll (3 x 24 = 72). The total yards is converted to feet by multiplying the number of yards by the number of feet in a yard (72 x 3 = 216).

20. a. Incorrect. You chose the number of feet per mile as the answer.

b. Incorrect. You divided the number of feet per mile by the number of miles.

c. Correct.

d. Incorrect.

Explanation: The number of feet is found by multiplying the number of miles by the number of feet in a mile (4.4 x 5,280 = 23,232).

21. a. Correct.

b. Incorrect.

Explanation: The number of feet needed is found by multiplying the distance in miles by the number of feet per mile (0.6 x 5,280 = 3,168). The 4,000 feet estimate is enough to cover the 3,168 feet actually needed.

22. a. Incorrect.

b. Correct.

Explanation: Multiply the number of feet in a mile by the number of miles (5,280 x 0.4 = 2,112). Reliable's cost is $3 per foot ($3 x 2,112 = $6,336). This offer is less than the $6,500 offer from Ace.

23. a. Correct.

b. Incorrect.

Explanation: The cost per yard for Outdoor Systems is found by multiplying the cost per foot by the conversion factor of ($1.50 x 3 = $4.50). Therefore, the $4.50 per yard bid is higher than the $4 per yard bid by Mercury Irrigation Systems.

24. a. Correct.

    b. Incorrect.

Explanation: The length in feet required for the two buildings is found by adding the lengths (12 yards, 2 feet, 9 inches + 38 yards, 1 foot, 8 inches = 50 yards, 3 feet, 17 inches which converts to 51 yards, 1 foot, 5 inches). Then convert the yards to feet (51 x 3 = 153). The 200 feet of wiring is enough.

25. a. Incorrect.

    b. Incorrect.

    c. Correct.

    d. Incorrect.

Explanation: The bid for the first company was $18,000. The bid for the second company was $15,312 (5.8 x 5,280 x $0.50 = $15,312—note that 5,280 feet equal 1 mile). The bid for the third company was $10,208 (5.8 x 1,760 x $1 = $10,208—note that 1,760 yards equal 1 mile). The third company offered the lowest bid.

SECTION 12: Weight

Quick Check

1. d	10. c	19. a
2. b	11. b	20. c
3. c	12. b	21. a
4. d	13. b	22. a
5. d	14. a	23. b
6. b	15. c	24. c
7. a	16. b	25. c
8. d	17. c	
9. a	18. b	

Explanations

Note the following conversion factors that will be useful for this section:

16 ounces =	1 pound
2,000 pounds =	1 ton

All answers should be converted to the highest form. For example, 20 ounces should be converted to 1 pound, 4 ounces.

1. d
2. b
3. c
4. d
5. d
6. a. Incorrect.
   b. Correct.
   c. Incorrect.
   d. Incorrect.

   Explanation: You could estimate that even a small computer would weigh more than 16 ounces, but less than 2,000 pounds. Therefore, the most likely unit of weight is pounds.

7. a. Correct.
   b. Incorrect.
   c. Incorrect.
   d. Incorrect.

   Explanation: The correct procedure to convert a measurement from ounces to pounds is to divide by 16 (the number of ounces in 1 pound). The number remaining represents ounces. For example, 35 ounces converts to 2 pounds, 3 ounces.

8. a. Incorrect. You added the number of ounces per tape to the number of tapes.
   b. Incorrect. You divided the number of tapes by the weight per tape.
   c. Incorrect. You followed the correct procedure, but did not convert the measurement to pounds.
   d. Correct.

Explanation: The total ounces is found by multiplying the number of items by the weight per item (20 x 4 = 80). Then, the number of ounces is divided by 16 to convert the measurement to pounds (80 / 16 = 5).

9. a. Correct.
   b. Incorrect. You subtracted the weight of the container from the weight of the copier.
   c. Incorrect. You multiplied the weight of the copier by 2.
   d. Incorrect.

   Explanation: The weight of the shipping container is added to the weight of the copier (10 pounds, 15 ounces + 1 pound, 3 ounces = 11 pounds, 18 ounces—which converts to 12 pounds, 2 ounces).

10. a. Incorrect. You divided the weight of the second package into the weight of the first package.
    b. Incorrect. You subtracted the weight of the second package from the weight of the first package.
    c. Correct.
    d. Incorrect.

    Explanation: Add the weight of the two packages to find the total weight (4 pounds, 14 ounces + 2 pounds, 7 ounces = 6 pounds, 21 ounces—which converts to 7 pounds, 5 ounces).

11. a. Incorrect.
    b. Correct.

    Explanation: Total approximate weight is determined by multiplying the approximate weight of each package by the number of packages (5 pounds, 8 ounces x 25 = 125 pounds, 200 ounces—which converts to 137 pounds, 8 ounces). This approximate weight is higher than the agreed total weight of 127 pounds.

12. a. Incorrect. You divided the total weight by 2.
    b. Correct.
    c. Incorrect. You multiplied the total weight by the number of reams.
    d. Incorrect. You added the total pounds to the total ounces.

    Explanation: The weight of each ream is found by dividing the total weight by the number of reams (16 pounds, 8 ounces / 8 = 2 pounds, 1 ounce).

13. a. Incorrect. You multiplied the total weight of the original shipment by the number of items.
    b. Correct.

c. Incorrect. You added the weight of the lost item to the total weight of the original shipment.

d. Incorrect.

Explanation: The weight of the remaining items is found by subtracting the weight of the lost item from the total weight of the original shipment (4 pounds, 5 ounces – 12 ounces = 3 pounds, 9 ounces).

14. a. Correct.

b. Incorrect.

Explanation: The total weight is found by multiplying the weight of each machine by the number of machines (1 pound, 8 ounces x 6 = 6 pounds, 48 ounces—which converts to 9 pounds). This is less than the 10 pounds maximum strength of the carton.

15. a. Incorrect.

b. Incorrect.

c. Correct.

d. Incorrect.

Explanation: The total weight is found by multiplying the weight per item by the number of items. Therefore, the weight per item is needed, but the number of employees is not necessary.

16. a. Incorrect.

b. Correct.

c. Incorrect.

d. Incorrect.

Explanation: The total weight is found by multiplying the weight per item by the number of items. Therefore, both the number of items and the weight per item are necessary to solve the problem.

17. a. Incorrect. You multiplied the number of hours per day by the number of items.

b. Incorrect. You multiplied the number of pounds by the number of items, but ignored the number of ounces.

c. Correct.

d. Incorrect. You added the weight per item to the number of items.

Explanation: The total weight of the order is found by multiplying the weight per item by the number of items (1 pound, 8 ounces x 200 = 200 pounds, 1600 ounces—which converts to 300 pounds).

18. a. Incorrect. You added the weight of the case to the weight of the computer with carrying case.

    b. Correct.

    c. Incorrect. You chose the weight of the computer with carrying case, without subtracting the weight of the case.

    d. Incorrect.

    Explanation: The weight of the case is subtracted to find the weight of the computer (22 pounds, 5 ounces - 15 ounces = 21 pounds, 6 ounces).

19. a. Correct.

    b. Incorrect.

    Explanation: The weight of the shipment is found by multiplying the weight per directory by the number of directories (1 pound, 8 ounces x 100 = 100 pounds, 800 ounces—which converts to 150 pounds). The cost for shipping by Quick Freight Company is found by multiplying the number of pounds by $1 (150 x $1 = $150). This amount is less than the $207 price agreed to by Express Today.

20. a. Incorrect.

    b. Incorrect.

    c. Correct.

    Explanation: Computations for the three orders are shown as follows: Quick Freight Company: 3 pounds, 8 ounces x 200 = 600 pounds, 1600 ounces—which converts to 700 pounds. Cost is found as follows: 700 x $.50 = $350. Express Today: $307. National Express: 200 x $1.50 = $300. Therefore, National Express offered the lowest price.

21. a. Correct.

    b. Incorrect.

    Explanation: First find the number of books each envelope can hold by dividing the envelope's capacity by the weight per book (5 pounds / 1 pound, 4 ounces = 4). If 4 books can be shipped in each envelope, find the number of envelopes needed by dividing the total number of books by the books per envelope (300 / 4 = 75). The 90 envelopes will be sufficient since only 75 envelopes are needed.

22. a. Correct.

    b. Incorrect.

Explanation: First convert 1 pound, 8 ounces to 1 1/2 pounds. Then, the number of bars is estimated by dividing the total weight of the order by the weight per bar (375 / 1 1/2 = 250). Therefore, the 250 estimate is reasonably close to the 248 bars actually ordered.

23. a. Incorrect. You divided the number of packages by the weight per package.
    b. Correct.
    c. Incorrect. You followed the correct procedure, but did not convert pounds to tons.
    d. Incorrect.

Explanation: The total weight of the packages is found by multiplying the number of packages by the weight per package (300 x 20 = 6,000). Divide by 2,000 to convert to tons (6,000 / 2,000 = 3).

24. a. Incorrect. You multiplied the weight by the number of trucks.
    b. Incorrect. You followed the correct procedure, but did not convert the number of pounds to tons.
    c. Correct.
    d. Incorrect.

Explanation: Add the weight of the asphalt on each truck to find the total weight (7,000 + 5,000 = 12,000). Divide by 2,000 to convert to 6 tons.

25. a. Incorrect. You divided the total weight by 1,000.
    b. Incorrect. You divided the maximum load by the number of deliveries.
    c. Correct.
    d. Incorrect.

Explanation: Total weight is found by multiplying the weight per load by the number of deliveries (7,000 x 14 = 98,000). Divide by 2,000 to convert to 49 tons.

SECTION 13: Combination Problems

Quick Check

1. c	10. d	19. a
2. d	11. a	20. a
3. b	12. d	21. b
4. a	13. c	22. c
5. b	14. b	23. b
6. c	15. b	24. a
7. c	16. c	25. a
8. c	17. a	
9. a	18. a	

Explanations

All answers should be converted to the highest form—minutes to hours, inches to feet, and so forth.

1. c
2. d
3. b
4. a
5. b
6. a. Incorrect. You added only the whole portion of each fraction.
   b. Incorrect. You included the rate per hour.
   c. Correct.
   d. Incorrect. You probably followed the correct procedure, but made an error while converting the portions of an hour to hours.

   Explanation: Add the number of hours worked to find total hours (5 1/4 + 6 1/2 + 4 3/4 = 16 1/2).

7. a. Incorrect. You included only the whole hour portion of the fraction.
   b. Incorrect. You made an error while converting to whole hours.
   c. Correct.
   d. Incorrect.

   Explanation: Total time billed is found by adding the time spent on each part of the job (5 1/2 + 6 1/4 + 3 1/2 = 15 1/4).

8. a. Incorrect. You omitted the minutes while computing your answer.
   b. Incorrect. You subtracted the hours required to transcribe the notes.

    c. Correct.

    d. Incorrect.

Explanation: Total time billed is found by adding the time worked each day (4 hours, 45 minutes + 5 hours, 30 minutes + 6 hours, 45 minutes = 15 hours, 120 minutes—which converts to 17 hours).

9. a. Correct.

    b. Incorrect.

Explanation: The required time to complete the job is determined by adding the time spent each day (4 hours + 6 hours, 45 minutes + 3 hours, 30 minutes = 13 hours, 75 minutes—which converts to 14 hours, 15 minutes or 14 1/4 hours). This was less than the 15 hours estimated time.

10. a. Incorrect. You found normal hours, but did not subtract the hours not worked on Thursday.

    b. Incorrect. You found normal hours, but added the number of hours not worked on Thursday.

    c. Incorrect. You followed the correct procedure, but made an error by not deducting 1 from 40 while subtracting the minutes left early on Thursday.

    d. Correct.

Explanation: Multiply the hours worked each day by the number of days (8 x 5 = 40). Then, subtract the time not worked from the normal hours worked to find actual hours worked (40 hours − 4 hours, 15 minutes = 35 hours, 45 minutes or 35 3/4 hours).

11. a. Correct.

    b. Incorrect. You added both the extra hours and the hours missed to the normal hours worked.

    c. Incorrect. You found only normal hours worked.

    d. Incorrect.

Explanation: First find the normal hours worked each week (8 x 5 = 40). Then add the extra hours worked on Monday and subtract the time missed on Wednesday from normal hours (40 + 3/4 − 1 1/2 = 39 1/4).

12. a. Incorrect. You chose the monthly payment amount.

    b. Incorrect. You included only the number of whole years required to repay the loan.

    c. Incorrect. You selected the number of months in a year as your answer.

    d. Correct.

Explanation: The number of years required to repay the loan is found by dividing the number of months by 12 (54 / 12 = 4.5 or 4 1/2 years).

13. a. Incorrect. You chose the number of weeks of vacation.

    b. Incorrect. You divided the number of weeks in a year by the number of weeks of vacation.

    c. Correct.

    d. Incorrect. You added the number of weeks of vacation to the number of weeks in a year.

Explanation: The number of weeks of vacation is subtracted from the total number of weeks in a year to find weeks worked (52 − 4 = 48).

14. a. Incorrect. Felicia worked exactly the same number of hours as the legal limit.

    b. Correct.

Explanation: The hours worked each day are added to find total hours worked (5 3/4 + 6 1/2 + 8 + 4 3/4 = 25). Then compare this amount to the legal limit.

15. a. Incorrect.

    b. Correct.

Explanation: Add to find the total length required (34 + 29 = 63). Then convert feet to yards (63 / 3 = 21). The 20 yards of cabling on the truck are not sufficient for the job.

16. a. Incorrect. You chose the total number of feet, without converting the measurement to yards.

    b. Incorrect. You subtracted the number of feet in a yard from the number of feet of cabling needed.

    c. Correct.

    d. Incorrect. You multiplied the number of feet of cabling needed by the number of feet in a yard.

Explanation: Divide by 3 to convert the measurement from feet to yards (54 / 3 = 18).

17. a. Correct.

    b. Incorrect.

Explanation: The amount of cloth needed is found by multiplying the number of yards needed for each uniform by the number of uniforms (5 4/5 x 5 = 29). The bolt of cloth is enough.

18. a. Correct.
    b. Incorrect. You multiplied the total area by the size of each sheet of plywood.
    c. Incorrect. You subtracted the size of each sheet of plywood from the total area to be roofed.
    d. Incorrect. You added the size of each sheet of plywood to the total area to be roofed.

    Explanation: The number of sheets needed is found by dividing the total area to be roofed by the area of each sheet of plywood (23,464 / 28 = 838).

19. a. Correct.
    b. Incorrect.

    Explanation: The total feet of fencing is found by multiplying the distance in miles by the number of feet in a mile (0.5 x 5,280 = 2,640). This distance is then multiplied by the cost per foot to determine the bid for Tri-State Fence Co. (2,640 x $4 = $10,560). This bid is greater than the $9,000 bid by Ole Town Fence Co.

20. a. Correct.
    b. Incorrect.

    Explanation: The number of yards is found by dividing the number of feet by 3 (1,500 / 3 = 500). The bid for City Systems is found by multiplying the number of yards by the $4 per yard bid price (500 x $4 = $2,000). This bid is $100 less than the bid by Nature Systems ($2,100 - $2,000 = $100).

21. a. Incorrect.
    b. Correct.
    c. Incorrect.
    d. Incorrect.

    Explanation: First convert the number of miles to yards by multiplying the number of miles by 1,760 (6.5 x 1,760 = 11,440). The bid by Nature Center is determined by multiplying the number of yards by the $1.50 bid price (11,440 x $1.50 = $17,160). The next step is to convert the number of miles to feet by multiplying the number of miles by 5,280 (6.5 x 5,280 = 34,320). The bid by Outdoors Unlimited is found by multiplying the number of feet by the $0.60 bid price (34,320 x $0.60 = $20,592). Therefore, the bid by Nature Center is the lowest and both bids are under the $25,000 budgeted amount.

22. a. Incorrect. You chose the number of radios.

   b. Incorrect. You chose the weight of each radio.

   c. Correct.

   d. Incorrect. You multiplied the number of ounces for all radios by the number of ounces in a pound.

Explanation: The total weight is found by multiplying the weight of each radio by the number of radios (14 ounces x 10 = 140). The number of ounces is divided by 16 to find the number of pounds (140 / 16 = 8.75 or 8 3/4 pounds).

23. a. Incorrect. You chose the total weight of the paper.

   b. Correct.

   c. Incorrect. You multiplied the total weight by the number of reams.

   d. Incorrect. You added the total weight to the number of reams.

Explanation: The weight of each ream is found by dividing the total weight by the number of reams (72 / 24 = 3).

24. a. Correct.

   b. Incorrect.

Explanation: The total weight is found by multiplying the weight of each calculator by the number of calculators (1 pound, 2 ounces x 18 = 18 pounds, 36 ounces—which converts to 20 pounds, 4 ounces). Therefore, the 24-pound strength is adequate.

25. a. Correct.

   b. Incorrect. You divided the number of packages by the weight per package.

   c. Incorrect. You chose the number of pounds in each ton as the alternative.

   d. Incorrect.

Explanation: Total weight is found by multiplying the weight of each package by the number of packages (80 x 350 = 28,000). Then, divide this number by the number of pounds in each ton to find the number of tons (28,000 / 2,000 = 14).

Extra Practice Exercises

Quick Check

1. a	13. b	25. a
2. b	14. b	26. b
3. c	15. c	27. a
4. c	16. a	28. a
5. d	17. b	29. b
6. a	18. b	30. c
7. b	19. d	31. b
8. c	20. a	32. b
9. c	21. b	33. b
10. c	22. b	34. a
11. a	23. c	35. b
12. b	24. b	

Explanations

1. a
2. b
3. c
4. c
5. d
6. a. Correct.
   b. Incorrect. You added the price quotes of the two stocks.
   c. Incorrect. You followed a procedure that was close to the correct one, but made an error while performing the subtraction operation.
   d. Incorrect. You just selected the price quote for the AMZ Corp. stock.

   Explanation: The difference in price quotes is found by subtracting the second price quote from the first price quote ($37.500 − $23.625 = $13.875).
7. a. Incorrect. You followed the correct procedure, but left off the sales amount for the last day.
   b. Correct.
   c. Incorrect. You added the dollar amounts, but did not include the cents in the addition process.
   d. Incorrect.

Explanation: The total sales amount is found by adding each daily sales amount ($123.45 + $143.89 + $189.50 + $139.42 + $120.51 = $716.77).

8. a. Incorrect. You found total earnings only.

   b. Incorrect. You found total deductions only.

   c. Correct.

   d. Incorrect. You added total deductions to total earnings.

   Explanation: The net pay is determined by (1) finding total earnings, (2) finding total deductions, and (3) subtracting total deductions from total earnings: (1) $592.54 + $83.59 = $676.13; (2) $44.25 + $109.25 = $153.50; (3) $676.13 − $153.50 = $522.63.

9. a. Incorrect. You selected the cost of the automobile.

   b. Incorrect. You did not subtract the sales commission amount.

   c. Correct. You added the sales commission amount.

   d. Incorrect. You subtracted the sales commission amount.

   Explanation: The loss amount is found by subtracting the sales price of the automobile from the original cost and adding the commission to the difference. ($10,218 − $8,935.58 + $200 = $1,482.42).

10. a. Incorrect. You found the profit for each bicycle.

    b. Incorrect. You found the profit for each bicycle and then divided by the number of bicycles.

    c. Correct.

    d. Incorrect. You added the cost price and the sales price to find profit for each bicycle, and then multiplied the sum by the number of bicycles.

    Explanation: First find the profit per bicycle by subtracting the cost price from the sales price ($235.84 − $175.24 = $60.60). Total profit is found by multiplying the profit per bicycle by the number of bicycles ($60.60 x 12 = $727.20).

11. a. Correct.

    b. Incorrect.

    Explanation: Multiply the number of chairs made per hour by the number of hours for each shift (8 x 8 = 64; 9 x 8 = 72). Then, add these values to find total chairs built during the two days (64 + 72 = 136). Since 136 chairs were built during the two days, he met and exceeded the company goal of 130 chairs.

12. a. Incorrect.
    b. Correct.

    Explanation: Multiply the cost per computer by the number of computers ($1,989 x 11 = $21,879). This amount exceeds the budgeted amount ($21,879 – $21,000 = $879), so the budget will not permit the purchase.

13. a. Incorrect. You added the number of records each day to the cost per record.
    b. Correct.
    c. Incorrect. You followed the correct procedure, but placed the decimal point one place too far to the right in your answer.
    d. Incorrect. You followed the correct procedure, but placed the decimal point one place too far to the left in your answer.

    Explanation: First find the daily data entry cost by multiplying the number of records by the cost per record (900 x $.085 = $76.50 and 400 x $.085 = $34). The cost for each day is added to find the cost for the job ($76.50 + $34 = $110.50).

14. a. Incorrect.
    b. Correct.

    Explanation: The first step is to find the total sales amount by multiplying the cost per membership by the number of memberships sold ($425 x 52 = $22,100). The commission amount is then found by multiplying the total sales amount by the commission rate ($22,100 x .015 = $331.50). This amount is larger than the $300 weekly salary.

15. a. Incorrect. You only found the cost of the legal pads.
    b. Incorrect. You only found the cost of the storage boxes.
    c. Correct.
    d. Incorrect. You subtracted the cost of the legal pads from the cost of the storage boxes.

    Explanation: Multiply the cost per item by the number of items ($.50 x 24 = $12 and $14.95 x 18 = $269.10). Add these amounts to the total amount of the bill ($12 + $269.10 = $281.10).

16. a. Correct.
    b. Incorrect. You included only the cost of the 144 disks ordered by the accounting department.
    c. Incorrect. You included only the cost of the 48 disks ordered by the finance department.

d. Incorrect. You used the price per box as the individual disk price.

Explanation: The cost per disk is found by dividing the cost per box by the number in each box ($18.60 / 12 = $1.55). The number of disks ordered is found by adding the number ordered by each department (144 + 48 = 192). Then multiply the cost per disk by the number of disks ordered ($1.55 x 192 = $297.60).

17. a. Incorrect.

b. Correct.

Explanation: Add the number of disks needed at each location (185 + 211 = 396). The number of dozen is found by dividing the number by 12—the number in a dozen (396 / 12 = 33). The 32 dozen disks that are in inventory are less than the 33 dozen disks needed.

18. a. Incorrect.

b. Correct.

c. Incorrect.

Explanation: Computations for each company are shown as follows. Crouch: 1,200 x $24.95 = $29,940. Smith: $30,000. Import: 500 x $32.85 = $16,425; 700 x $27.50 = $19,250; $16,425 + $19,250 = $35,675. Therefore, Crouch Office Supply offered the lowest price ($29,940).

19. a. Incorrect. You used the savings as the part and overtime earnings as the whole while developing the fraction.

b. Incorrect. You used rental expenses as the part and regular earnings as the whole while developing the fraction.

c. Incorrect. You used savings as the part and regular earnings as the whole while developing the fraction.

d. Correct.

Explanation: First find total income by adding regular earnings to overtime earnings ($20,000 + $4,000 = $24,000). The $2,000 is the part of the fraction, the $24,000 is the whole ($2,000/$24,000). Then, the fraction is reduced to lowest terms ($2,000/$24,000 = 1/12).

20. a. Correct.

b. Incorrect. You made the comparison for the freshman class only.

c. Incorrect. You made the comparison for the sophomore class only.

d. Incorrect.

Explanation: The number of total applicants accepted is found by adding the number of applicants accepted for each class (400 + 300 = 700). Then add the number of applicants for each class (600 + 400 = 1,000). The fraction is written with the number of applicants accepted as the part and the total applicants as the whole (700/1,000 = 7/10).

21. a. Incorrect.

    b. Correct.

Explanation: The partnership profit is multiplied by the fraction allocated to Mr. Benz (1/3) to find his share ($144,000 x 1/3 = $48,000). Since this amount is larger than the $46,000 amount, Mr. Benz's best option is to receive 1/3 of the partnership profit as his share.

22. a. Incorrect.

    b. Correct.

Explanation: First find the total hours worked by adding the hours worked each day (7 1/2 + 6 1/4 + 7 3/4 + 6 3/4 = 28 1/4). Total pay is then found by multiplying the hours worked by the hourly pay rate (28 1/4 x $8.60 = $242.95). This amount is larger than the $225 weekly earnings amount.

23. a. Incorrect. You found the total price of the word processors, without the discount.

    b. Incorrect. You determined the discount on only 1 word processor.

    c. Correct.

    d. Incorrect. You divided the price per word processor by the discount percent.

Explanation: Multiply the price per word processor by the number of word processors ($270 x 4 = $1,080). The discount is then found by multiplying the total price by the discount rate ($1,080 x .3 = $324).

24. a. Incorrect. You followed the correct procedure, but placed the decimal point one place too far to the right in your answer.

    b. Correct.

    c. Incorrect. You divided the total operating expenses by the rental equipment amount.

    d. Incorrect. You treated the rental equipment portion as an amount instead of as a percent of total expenses.

Explanation: Divide the amount allocated to rental equipment by the total operating expenses to find the percent allocated to rental equipment ($1,200 / $4,800 = .25 or 25 percent).

25. a. Correct.
    b. Incorrect.

    Explanation: The amount of raise is found by multiplying the annual salary by the raise percent ($38,500 x .125 = $4,812.50). His salary after the raise is found by adding his annual salary to the raise amount ($38,500 + $4,812.50 = $43,312.50). Since this amount is larger than the $42,000 offered by the competing company, Paul will earn a higher salary with his present company.

26. a. Incorrect.
    b. Correct.

    Explanation: The percent of defective products is found by dividing the number of defective parts by the total number of completed parts (6/300 = .02 or 2 percent). This percent is higher than the 1 percent acceptable standard.

27. a. Correct.
    b. Incorrect. You divided the number of chips presently being produced by the number of present technicians.
    c. Incorrect. You used an incorrect proportion 20/800:1,000/?.
    d. Incorrect. You divided the number of products to be produced with increased production by the number of present technicians.

    Explanation: The relationship between 20 technicians producing 800 chips and an unknown number of technicians producing 1,000 chips is 20/800:?/1,000. This proportion provides a value of 25 (800 x ? = 20,000 or ? = 25).

28. a. Correct.
    b. Incorrect.

    Explanation: Multiply the monthly income amount by the number of months in a year ($3,000 x 12 = $36,000). Then divide the mortgage amount by the annual income ($84,000 / $36,000 = 2 1/3). Since this relationship is less than the 2 1/2 general rule, the client will qualify for the $84,000 mortgage amount.

29. a. Incorrect. You followed the correct procedure, but placed the decimal point one place too far to the right in your answer.
    b. Correct.
    c. Incorrect. You followed the correct procedure, but placed the decimal point one place too far to the left in your answer.
    d. Incorrect. You followed the correct procedure, but did not convert the decimal value to a percent.

Explanation: Divide the bonus amount by the sales amount ($735 / $42,000 = 0.0175 or 1.75 percent).

30. a. Incorrect. You found the total hours worked during the week and then converted it to a dollar amount.
    b. Incorrect. You chose the hourly rate as your answer.
    c. Correct.
    d. Incorrect. You followed the correct procedure, but placed the decimal point one place too far to the right in your answer.

Explanation: Add the hours worked each day (7 3/4 + 7 1/2 + 8 + 7 1/4 + 8 = 38 1/2). Then, multiply by the hourly rate to find weekly earnings (38 1/2 x $12.50 = $481.25).

31. a. Incorrect.
    b. Correct.

Explanation: EZ: First find the number of months in 3 1/2 years (3 1/2 x 12 = 42), then, determine total payments ($350 x 42 = $14,700). Best: First find the number of weeks in 3 1/2 years (3 1/2 x 52 = 182), then, determine total payments ($80 x 182 = $14,560). The weekly plan offered by Best Deal Auto Sales provides the lowest total payments.

32. a. Incorrect.
    b. Correct.

Explanation: Add the number of feet needed for both rooms (37 + 59 = 96). Then, divide by 3 to find the total number of yards needed (96 / 3 = 32). The 30 yards on the truck are not enough to do the job requiring 32 yards.

33. a. Incorrect.
    b. Correct.
    c. Incorrect.

Explanation: Design: Find the number of feet in 1.5 miles (1.5 x 5,280 = 7,920). Then, determine the cost at $3.50 per foot (7,920 x $3.50 = $27,720). Safenet: First find the number of yards in 1.5 miles (1.5 x 1,760 = 2,640). Then, find the cost at $10 per yard (2,640 x $10 = $26,400). AAA: $27,000 agreed price. Safenet offered the lowest of the three prices, $26,400.

34. a. Correct.

    b. Incorrect.

    Explanation: Multiply the number of items by the weight per item (200 x 2 pounds, 4 ounces = 400 pounds, 800 ounces, which converts to 450 pounds). Then, find the shipping cost offered by Champion Freight Services by multiplying the number of pounds by the cost per pound (450 x $0.75 = $337.50). This amount is lower than the $350 price offered by Express Now.

35. a. Incorrect. You chose the price for 1 load.

    b. Correct.

    c. Incorrect. You chose the price for 3 loads.

    d. Incorrect. You chose the price for 4 loads.

    Explanation: Find the total weight of the packages by multiplying the number of packages by the weight per package (300 x 35 pounds = 10,500 pounds). Then, find the number of tons by dividing the total pounds by the number of pounds per ton (10,500 / 2,000 = 5.25). Since the truck capacity is 3 tons, delivery of 5.25 tons can be made in 2 loads. The delivery charge is computed by multiplying the number of loads by the price per load (2 x 100 = $200).

UNIT I TEST: Answer Sheet

• •

1. _____
2. _____
3. _____
4. _____
5. _____
6. _____
7. _____
8. _____
9. _____
10. _____
11. _____
12. _____
13. _____
14. _____
15. _____
16. _____
17. _____
18. _____
19. _____
20. _____
21. _____
22. _____
23. _____
24. _____
25. _____

UNIT II TEST: Answer Sheet

1. _____
2. _____
3. _____
4. _____
5. _____
6. _____
7. _____
8. _____
9. _____
10. _____
11. _____
12. _____
13. _____
14. _____
15. _____
16. _____
17. _____
18. _____
19. _____
20. _____
21. _____
22. _____
23. _____
24. _____
25. _____

UNIT III TEST: Answer Sheet

1. _____
2. _____
3. _____
4. _____
5. _____
6. _____
7. _____
8. _____
9. _____
10. _____
11. _____
12. _____
13. _____
14. _____
15. _____
16. _____
17. _____
18. _____
19. _____
20. _____
21. _____
22. _____
23. _____
24. _____
25. _____